MW00641326

Living in the
MILLENNIUM

ALSO BY ROBERT L. MILLET

Living in the
MILLENNIUM

ROBERT L. MILLET

DESERET
BOOK

Salt Lake City, Utah

Library of Congress Cataloging-in-Publication Data

CIP data on file

ISBN 978-1-60907-914-7

Printed in Canada

Friesens, Manitoba, Canada

10 9 8 7 6 5 4 3 2 1

The wolf also shall dwell with the lamb, and the leopard shall lie down with the kid; and the calf and the young lion and the fatling together; and a little child shall lead them. They shall not hurt nor destroy in all my holy mountain: for the earth shall be full of the knowledge of the Lord, as the waters cover the sea.

ISAIAH 11:6, 9

The hour is nigh, and that which was spoken by mine apostles must be fulfilled; for as they spoke so shall it come to pass; for I will reveal myself from heaven with power and great glory, with all the hosts thereof, and dwell in righteousness with men on earth a thousand years, and the wicked shall not stand.

DOCTRINE & COVENANTS 29:10–11

CONTENTS

PREFACE

For many years, beginning long before I began the research for this project, I have often found myself singing or whistling two favorite hymns, the words of which have simply become a part of me. The first hymn beckons to each one of us:

> *Come, let us anew our journey pursue,*
> *Roll round with the year,*
> *And never stand still till the Master appear.*
> *His adorable will let us gladly fulfill,*
> *And our talents improve,*
> *By the patience of hope and the labor of love.*
>
> *Our life as a dream, our time as a stream*
> *Glide swiftly away,*
> *And the fugitive moment refuses to stay;*
> *For the arrow is flown and the moments are gone.*
> *The millennial year*
> *Presses on to our view, and eternity's here.*[1]

The other hymn is one that moves me to the core and creates a feeling of sweet anticipation for a time and a day grander than the present:

Jehovah, Lord of heaven and earth,
Thy word of truth proclaim!
Oh, may it spread from pole to pole,
Till all shall know thy name.

We long to see thy Church increase,
Thine own new kingdom grow,
That all the earth may live in peace,
And heav'n be seen below.

Roll on thy work in all its pow'r!
The distant nations bring!
In thy new kingdom may they stand,
And own thee God and King.

One general chorus then shall rise
From men of ev'ry tongue,
And songs of joy salute the skies,
By ev'ry nation sung.[2]

I love the music of these two grand anthems, to be sure, but it is the words that stir my soul and motivate me to live better than I do now, that remind me that today is a day of preparation for a greater time. Those amazing words point us toward a day when the Lord Jesus will come down and be with us, when the Christ will dwell among his people, when the Savior will transform this fallen earth into a paradisiacal world.

Living in the Millennium is the sequel to *Living in the Eleventh Hour* (Deseret Book, 2014). In that study, we discussed many of the signs of the times, events that will take place and attitudes that will exist in the years leading up to the Second Coming, the knowledge of which can do much to prepare each of us for that great and dreadful day. We spoke of such things as men's hearts failing them, false Christs and false prophets, standing in holy places, preaching the gospel to all the world, the gathering of Israel, wars and rumors of wars, the fall of the great and abominable church, and the establishment of the New Jerusalem. Our intent in that volume was to undertake a serious study of the times and doings of those days leading up to the Savior's glorious appearance.

In this companion volume, we will begin by looking more closely at what we have come to call Christ's preliminary appearances, that is, private comings of the Master to selected groups before he appears to all people. Then we will turn to the scriptures and the prophetic word to discover what it will be like when the lowly Nazarene returns in majesty and power to cleanse the earth by fire, remove wickedness and wicked people, and initiate a thousand years of goodness and peace. If there is anything in my research for this project that has surprised me, it is how extensively the prophets have spoken of life on the millennial earth and of the grand events that will unfold when Satan no longer has power over the hearts of our Heavenly Father's children. God and his anointed servants have spoken in remarkable detail of this transcendent and delightful time. Then we will turn our attention to the resurrection and the day of judgment that every man, woman, and child will experience as they are called upon to render an account of how they have spent their time and expended their resources during their second estate. Finally, we will bask in the light of the marvelous revelations that unfold to our view the nature of life in the kingdoms of glory hereafter. It is an amazing journey, an exciting and sacred education.

One of the themes running through both books is encouragement to face the future soberly but optimistically. "We live in troubled times—very troubled times," President Boyd K. Packer said. "We hope, we pray, for better days. But that is not to be.

The prophecies tell us that. We will not as a people, as families, or as individuals be exempt from the trials to come. No one will be spared the trials common to home and family, work, disappointment, grief, health, aging, ultimately death.

"What then shall we do? . . . We need not live in fear of the future. We have every reason to rejoice and little reason to fear. If we follow the promptings of the Spirit, we will be safe, whatever the future holds. We will be shown what to do."[3]

On another occasion President Packer taught simply. "Fear and faith are antagonistic to one another, and it is our obligation to promote faith, not fear; so stand steady."[4]

Like *Living in the Eleventh Hour*, this work is a private endeavor and not an official publication of The Church of Jesus Christ of Latter-day Saints or Brigham Young University, where I worked for some thirty years and where this project was begun and completed. Although I have sought, perhaps even more than with any other book I have ever written, to be in harmony with holy scripture and the teachings of latter-day prophets, I alone am responsible for the conclusions drawn from the evidence cited.

Chapter 1

THE END OF TIME

I was driving to work one day and turned the radio to an oldies channel, where I heard a familiar song from the 1960s, a tender ballad, a love song. Over and over the artist sang of love lasting until the end of time. Later that afternoon I listened to the same channel and heard another artist pledging his love until time stood still. I smiled as I reflected on the message of those two popular songs, realizing how very often such sentiments are sung or how frequently a romantic sentiment is expressed in just that way. I presume the writers of these words intended to convey some meaning like "I'll love you forever and ever" or "There will never be a time when I no longer love you."

The more I have thought about it, the more fully I realize that from a Restoration perspective, love is intended to last longer than time, to span the veil of death and continue everlastingly. For those without such understanding, however, "till time stands still" or "to the end of time" seems like a pretty significant and long-term investment of one's love. Let's consider this passage of scripture: "And the angel which I saw stand upon the sea and upon the earth lifted up his hand to heaven, and sware by him that liveth for ever and ever, who created heaven, and the things that therein are, and the earth, and the things that therein are, and the sea, and the things which are therein, that *there should be time no longer*" (Revelation 10:5–6; emphasis added; see D&C 88:108–10).

As a part of the new song that is to be sung by the redeemed are these words:

> The Lord hath brought again Zion;
> The Lord hath redeemed his people, Israel,
> According to the election of grace,
> Which was brought to pass by the faith
> And covenant of their fathers.
> The Lord hath redeemed his people;
> And Satan is bound and *time is no longer*.
> (D&C 84:99–100; emphasis added)

We are told in the Doctrine and Covenants that "it is required of the Lord, at the hand of every steward, to render an account of his stewardship, both in time and in eternity. For he who is faithful and wise in time is accounted worthy to inherit the mansions prepared for him of my Father" (D&C 72:3–4).

I presume there will always be what might be called durational time, the fact that event A took place before event B, or that we declared C before we uttered D. What the scriptures seem to be saying, however, when they speak of time being no longer is that mortal time, or mortality, will be no longer. That is, a day is coming in the not too distant future when mortality as we know it will be no more; we will no longer be reckoning our words and our actions according to this world's calendar but rather we will be tuned and acclimated to eternity.

We have been counseled by the prophets to improve our time, that is, to make wise and effective use of the day in which we live on earth, for how we will spend *eternity* will be inextricably linked to how we spent our *time* in this life. And so we are told that "this life is the time for men to prepare to meet God; yea, behold the day of this life is the day for men to perform their labors" (Alma 34:32).

What will life be like when mortal time is no more? We can learn from holy scripture and latter-day apostles and prophets about the following:

- the private appearances of Jesus Christ to his anointed servants;
- that great and terrible day we know as the Savior's coming in glory;
- the cleansing of the earth by fire and the transformation of the planet;
- life on a terrestrial earth;
- a day when the gathering of Israel, accomplished through our missionary labors, will be unhindered and thus accelerated;
- a glorious time when temples will dot the earth and the fulness of the blessings of the house of the Lord will be enjoyed by the pure in heart in every nation;
- a time when persons will again begin to deny their God, when Satan will be loosed for a short season;
- when the final great battle between good and evil will take place;
- the miracle and wonder of our resurrection from the dead;
- the day of judgment, when all will be required to account for how they handled their stewardship of time; and,
- life within the kingdoms of glory, the many mansions of the Father.

Concerning the specifics of the future, details do matter, but they need to come from the right source—from holy scripture or from latter-day apostles and prophets. For me or for any other writer or teacher to go beyond what ancient or modern prophets have declared, to set forth private views concerning the last days, whether based upon individual interpretations or personal spiritual experience, is to assume a responsibility that is not ours; it is to act outside our stewardship. The ideas may be fascinating, even entertaining, but they are not from God; the Lord simply does not operate that way. To do so would be to invite every member of the Church to step forward, offer his or her own best guess about the days ahead, and thereby engender chaos. The Lord's house is a house of order, not a house of confusion. There are channels to follow, and we must recognize those channels. Therein is our safety from deception. The Prophet Joseph Smith stated the principle as follows: "I will inform you that it is contrary to the economy of God for any member of the Church, or any one, to receive instruction for those in authority, higher than themselves; therefore *you will see the impropriety of giving heed to them*; but if any person have a vision or a visitation from a heavenly messenger, it must be for his own benefit and instruction; for the fundamental principles, government, and doctrine of the Church are vested in the keys of the kingdom."[1]

I have therefore chosen to quote more extensively from holy scripture and from the writings and sermons of apostles and prophets than I am generally accustomed to doing. Although I do not wish to burden the reader with excessive support and substantiation, I do want to be as doctrinally sound and as loyal to the Lord's anointed as I can.

Operating in harmony with such restraint, let us proceed on our journey. And what a journey it will be! What an encounter will be ours as we make our way through the prophetic word and contemplate the glories that await the true and faithful. Looking to the future will do much to motivate us to get our lives in order while we are still living in time, for eternity is just around the corner. In addition, a view of the future can fortify us against the discouragement that inevitably follows from the pain and distresses of this fallen world; it provides us with a perspective that produces gospel gladness.

Chapter 2

THE SAVIOR'S PRELIMINARY APPEARANCES

*N*ot long ago I was invited to speak to a group of single adults in a distant stake. I attended the local ward that Sunday morning. In the Gospel Doctrine class, our topic was the signs of the times, and, as one might expect, the conversation was lively and quite fascinating. Some of the members of the class referred to several of the signs of the times given by Jesus on the Mount of Olives (see Joseph Smith–Matthew; D&C 45, 88, 133). They then linked various signs with actual events that had either recently taken place or that seemed to be apt descriptions of what was happening in the world at that very time. It was a sobering conversation that continued for about thirty minutes. One class member then got our attention by suggesting that the Millennium had actually begun early in the twentieth century; another disagreed, stating with fervor that the Millennium would gradually come to pass because individuals would eventually follow the teachings in the Sermon on the Mount. A class that had begun on a high note ended in debate and a great deal of confusion.

Once in a while we hear that not everyone will know when the Lord returns. Let's be clear on this matter. It will not be necessary for you to run to the phone and call Aunt Bertha to inform her that the Millennium has begun. The ward newsletter will probably not contain an announcement of the same. I rather suspect that it will not be necessary to watch the evening news to confirm rumors that are circulating in the city.

At the end of the eighteenth century, a woman by the name of Ann Lee claimed to have received a revelation in which she learned that she was the "feminine principle," or expression, of Jesus Christ and that the Second Coming had taken place through her ministry to the earth. The word spread and disciples were made, and a religious order known as the United Society of Believers in Christ's Second Appearing (also known as the Shaking Quakers or the Shakers) came into being. By the early nineteenth century, members of the Society could be found in America, and a branch had been formed near Cleveland, Ohio. A Shaker by the name of Leman Copley encountered missionaries of The Church of Jesus Christ of Latter-day Saints and was converted to the restored gospel. The Prophet Joseph received a revelation concerning the Shakers and instructed Sidney Rigdon, Parley P. Pratt, and Leman Copley to travel to the Shaker community in North Union, Ohio, and read the revelation to Shaker leaders. The Lord explained that "the Son of Man cometh not in the form of a woman, neither of a man traveling on the earth." Very pertinent counsel followed: "Wherefore, be not deceived, but continue in steadfastness, looking forth for the heavens to be shaken, and the earth to tremble and reel to and fro as a drunken man, and for the valleys to be exalted, and for the mountains to be made low, and for the rough places to become smooth—and all this when the angel shall sound his trumpet" (D&C 49:23). In short, everyone will know when the King of kings and Lord of lords descends from heaven with a shout (1 Thessalonians 4:16). It won't be a secret.

HE COMES TO HIS TEMPLE

It might be wise to speak of the second *comings* of the Lord Jesus Christ, some of which are preliminary appearances or comings to selected groups. First, the Lord will make a preliminary appearance to his temple in Independence, Jackson County, Missouri. Malachi prophesied in about 400 b.c.: "Behold, I will send my messenger, and he shall prepare the way before me: and the Lord, whom ye seek, shall suddenly come to his temple, even the messenger of the covenant, whom ye delight in: behold, he shall come, saith the Lord of hosts" (Malachi 3:1). One fulfillment of this prophecy was certainly the coming of John the Baptist, the one sent of the Father to prepare the way for the Promised Messiah. The Lord Jesus Christ came to his temple in the sense that he came to this earth on his mission of mercy. He also came to his temple in that he came to the temple of Herod and there taught the gospel with power and persuasion and confronted the hypocrisy of the scribes and Pharisees.

A later fulfillment of that prophecy occurred in this dispensation, the dispensation of the fulness of times: The restoration of the gospel, including the call and empowerment of modern apostles and prophets, began the formal preparation for the second coming of the Master. In our day the Savior declared: "I have sent mine everlasting covenant"—the fulness of the gospel of Jesus Christ—"into the world, to be a light to the world, and to be a standard for my people, and for the Gentiles to seek to it, and *to be a messenger before my face to prepare the way before me*" (D&C 45:9; emphasis added).

"Where, then, will the Lord come," Elder Bruce R. McConkie

asked, "in what places will he stand, and whence shall his voice
be heard? The Lord, whom we seek, shall suddenly come to his
temple, meaning that he will come to the earth, which is his
temple, and also that he will come to those holy houses which
he has commanded us to build unto his blessed name. Indeed, he
came suddenly to the Kirtland Temple on the 3rd day of April in
1836; he has also appeared in others of his holy houses; and he
will come in due course to the temples in Jackson County and
in Jerusalem. And he will come to his American Zion and his
Jewish Jerusalem. His voice will roar forth from both world capitals. He will speak personally, angelic ministrants will proclaim
his word, and his mortal servants will speak with his voice. . . .
The clear meaning is that there will be many appearances, in
many places, to many people."[1]

This coming of the Savior to his temple seems to be a private appearance to those holding the keys of power in the earthly
kingdom. Elder Orson Pratt, in speaking of this appearance, said:
"All of them who are pure in heart will behold the face of the
Lord and that too before he comes in his glory in the clouds of
heaven, for he will suddenly come to his Temple, and he will purify the sons of Moses and of Aaron, until they shall be prepared
to offer in that Temple an offering that shall be acceptable in
the sight of the Lord [see Malachi 3:3; D&C 13; 84:31]. In doing this, he will purify not only the minds of the Priesthood in
that Temple, but he will purify their bodies until they shall be
quickened, renewed and strengthened, and they will be partially
changed, not to immortality, but changed in part that they can
be filled with the power of God, and they can stand in the presence of Jesus, and behold his face in the midst of that Temple."[2]

President Charles W. Penrose observed that the Lord "will
come to the Temple prepared for him, and his faithful people will

behold his face, hear his voice, and gaze upon his glory. From his own lips they will receive further instructions for the development and beautifying of Zion and for the extension and sure stability of his Kingdom."[3]

HE COMES TO ADAM-ONDI-AHMAN

The Lord will then appear at Adam-ondi-Ahman, "the place where Adam shall come to visit his people, or the Ancient of Days shall sit" (D&C 116:1). This grand council will be the occasion for a large sacrament meeting, a time when the Son of Man will partake of the fruit of the vine once more with his earthly friends. And who will be in attendance? The revelations specify Moroni, Elias, John the Baptist, Elijah, Abraham, Isaac, Jacob, Joseph, Adam, Peter, James, John, "and also," the Savior tells us, "all those whom my Father hath given me out of the world" (D&C 27:5–14), multitudes of faithful Saints from the beginning of time to the end.

This will be a private appearance in that it will be unknown to the world. It will be a leadership meeting, a time of accounting for priesthood stewardships. The Prophet Joseph Smith explained that Adam, the Ancient of Days, "will call his children together and hold a council with them to prepare them for the coming of the Son of Man. He (Adam) is the father of the human family, and presides over the spirits of all men, and all that have had the keys must stand before him in this grand council. . . . The Son of Man stands before him, and there is given him [Christ] glory and dominion. Adam delivers up his stewardship to Christ, that which was delivered to him as holding the keys of the universe, but retains his standing as head of the human family."[4]

President Joseph Fielding Smith observed: "This gathering of the children of Adam, where the thousands, and the tens of thousands are assembled in the judgment, will be one of the greatest events this troubled earth has ever seen. At this conference, or council, all who have held keys of dispensations will render a report for their stewardship. . . . We do not know how long a time this gathering will be in session, or how many sessions will be held at this grand council. It is sufficient to know that it is a gathering of the Priesthood of God from the beginning of this earth down to the present, in which reports will be made and all who have been given dispensations (talents) will declare their keys and ministry and make report of their stewardship according to the parable [the parable of the talents; Matthew 25]. Judgment will be rendered unto them for this is a gathering of the righteous. . . . It is not to be the judgment of the wicked. . . . This will precede the great day of destruction of the wicked and will be the preparation for the Millennial Reign."[5]

In short, Adam "comes to set in order the councils of the Priesthood pertaining to all dispensations, to arrange the Priesthood and the councils of the Saints of all former dispensations in one grand family and household." For what purpose? "It is to prepare the way for another august personage whom Daniel saw coming with the clouds of heaven, namely the Son of Man."[6] How this is to be accomplished, how all of these priesthood holders and legal administrators are to be in attendance, has not been revealed, but given what we are able to do even in our own time, in terms of satellite communication, it is not impossible to conceive of such a gathering.

HE COMES TO THE MOUNT OF OLIVES

The Savior will appear to the Jews on the Mount of Olives. It will be at the time of the battle of Armageddon, a time when his people will find themselves with their backs against the wall.

During this period, two prophets will stand before the wicked in the streets of Jerusalem and call the people to repentance. These two men, presumably members of the Council of the Twelve Apostles or the First Presidency of The Church of Jesus Christ of Latter-day Saints, "are to be raised up to the Jewish nation in the last days, at the time of the restoration," and will "prophesy to the Jews after they are gathered and have built the city of Jerusalem in the land of their fathers" (D&C 77:15; see also Revelation 11:4–6).[7] They will be put to death by their enemies, their bodies will lie in the streets for three and a half days, and they will then be resurrected before the assembled multitude (Revelation 11:7–12).

At about this time, the Savior will come to the rescue of his covenant people: "Then shall the Lord go forth, and fight against those nations, as when he fought in the day of battle. And his feet shall stand in that day upon the mount of Olives, which is before Jerusalem on the east, and the mount of Olives shall cleave in the midst thereof toward the east and toward the west, and there shall be a very great valley; and half of the mountain shall remove toward the north, and half of it toward the south" (Zechariah 14:3–4). Then shall come to pass the conversion of a nation in a day, the acceptance of their Messiah by the Jews. "And then shall the Jews look upon me and say: What are these wounds in thine hands and in thy feet? Then shall they know that I am the Lord; for I will say unto them: These wounds are the wounds with which I was wounded in the house of my friends. I am he who was lifted up. I am Jesus that was crucified. I am the Son of God. And then shall they weep because of their iniquities; then shall they lament because they persecuted their king" (D&C 45:51–53; see also Zechariah 12:10; 13:6).

Many of us can recall vividly participating in a church

meeting or conference session that really made a difference in our lives. Perhaps it was something said in a particular talk, some poignant testimony that was borne, or something we felt as we left the gathering. President Gordon B. Hinckley remembered attending a stake priesthood meeting as a deacon in the Aaronic Priesthood in which he stood with the other boys and men in the chapel as they sang the opening hymn, "Praise to the Man Who Communed with Jehovah." "The chapel rang with the words of that great hymn," President Hinckley observed. "It was sung with conviction and intensity by men who carried in their hearts a powerful testimony of the prophetic calling of him of whom they sang.

"I have never forgotten that moment in my life. I was an awkward, freckled-faced little boy in knee pants, more prone to laugh than to be serious. But on this occasion, I felt a great moving power. It was both emotional and spiritual. Ever since, that hymn has held a special place in my heart, and its testimony has become my own testimony."[8]

Interestingly enough, decades later I attended a general priesthood meeting in our stake center, a meeting in which Gordon B. Hinckley, then the President of the Church, delivered the concluding message to the brethren gathered in stake centers throughout the world. The meeting prior to the concluding talk had for me been phenomenal; each speaker seemed to know just what I needed desperately to hear, what comfort and consolation and direction would be as manna to my troubled soul. And then President Hinckley spoke. It was one of those times—no doubt very much like the occasion of which he himself spoke—in which light and pure intelligence flooded the room. The living oracle and mouthpiece for the Almighty gave voice to the sentiments of Him who guides this Church. President Hinckley spoke with a power that I felt was unusual even for him. I wept through much of the closing hymn and prayer. After amen was said and we began to leave the church, I noticed how sober and solemn the mood was among the men of the stake, not a fearful or frightful soberness but a sweet and stirring realization that we had just left a hallowed presence. One older high priest walking with a friend just ahead of me broke the silence with these words: "Gordon B. Hinckley just spoke with the tongue of angels." I nodded my head in complete agreement, as did several others all around me.

Wonderful things have happened in days past in assemblies of the Saints. And things even more wonderful than words can describe will yet take place. When I think of what is to come, and particularly as I contemplate the great council at Adam-ondi-Ahman, it occurs to me that the best preparation you and I can make here and now to prepare for there and then is to magnify our callings, fulfill our assignments with caring consistency, and thus be in a position to give a positive report in sessions of accountability that will take place either here or hereafter.

We have been instructed that "it is required of the Lord, at the hand of every steward, to render an account of his stewardship, both in time and in eternity. For he who is faithful and wise in time is accounted worthy to inherit the mansions prepared for him of my Father" (D&C 72:3–4; see also 51:19; 78:22). To the extent that in this life I can sit with my family in the bishop's office annually and declare myself as a full-tithe payer, to that extent I will be well on my way to enjoying the riches of eternity in the life to come. To the extent that I am regular and consistent in strengthening those families assigned to me now as a home teacher (see D&C 20:53), to that extent my moments of accounting many years from now will be sweet and satisfying. To the extent that I assume rightful responsibility for family home evenings, family prayers, and family scripture study, to that extent my time of accounting for my stewardship in eternity will be exciting and exhilarating.

Soberly I acknowledge that one day I will stand before God and be required to give an accounting for how I have loved and cared for my wife and children, how I have nurtured them, how I have blessed them by and through the priesthood, how I have sought to teach them the gospel and prepare them to be faithful citizens in the kingdom of God and the community of man. I likely will not be asked to show my stocks and portfolios, to display my mortal medals, or to highlight my occupational achievements, but I *will* be expected to answer for how I have overseen the growth and development of the most important unit in time and eternity—my family. When I think of these things, I want to be better than I am. When I reflect on what lies ahead, I yearn to avoid being caught up in the thick of thin things, to find contentment in the simple pleasures that inevitably bring the deepest joys, and to recognize the moments that matter and make the most of them.

Chapter 3

JESUS CHRIST COMES IN GLORY

$\mathcal{J}$esus came to earth as a mortal being in the meridian of time. He taught the gospel, bestowed divine authority, organized the Church, and suffered and died as an infinite atoning sacrifice for the sins of the world. He taught that he would come again, not as the meek and lowly Nazarene but as the Lord of Sabaoth, the Lord of Hosts, the Lord of armies. His second coming is thus spoken of as his coming in glory, meaning, in his true identity as the God of all creation, the Redeemer and Judge.

THE END OF WICKEDNESS

When the Lord returns in glory, every corruptible thing will be destroyed. "The presence of the Lord shall be as the melting fire that burneth, and as fire which causeth the waters to boil. And so great shall be the glory of his presence that the sun shall hide his face in shame, and the moon shall withhold its light, and the stars shall be hurled from their places" (D&C 133:41, 49).

It will be a selective burning, for those who are of a celestial or a terrestrial state will abide the day; all else will be cleansed from the surface of the earth. Those who lie and cheat and steal, those who revel in immorality and pervert the ways

17

of righteousness, those who mock and point the finger of scorn at the Saints of the Most High—all these will be burned at his coming, and their spirits will take up residence in the spirit world, there to await the last resurrection at the end of a thousand years. The second coming in glory is "the end of the world," meaning the end of the worldly, the destruction of the wicked (Joseph Smith–Matthew 1:4).

The prophet Nephi wrote: "The time cometh speedily that Satan shall have no more power over the hearts of the children of men; for the day soon cometh that all the proud and they who do wickedly shall be as stubble; and the day cometh that they must be burned. For the time soon cometh that the fulness of the wrath of God shall be poured out upon all the children of men; for he will not suffer that the wicked shall destroy the righteous. Wherefore, *he will preserve the righteous by his power,* even if it so be that the fulness of his wrath must come, and the righteous be preserved, *even unto the destruction of their enemies by fire.* Wherefore, the righteous need not fear; for thus saith the prophet, they shall be saved, even if it so be as by fire" (1 Nephi 22:15–17; emphasis added; compare Malachi 4:1).

Nephi added that "the time speedily shall come that all churches which are built up to get gain, and all those who are built up to get power over the flesh, and those who are built up to become popular in the eyes of the world, and those who seek the lusts of the flesh and the things of the world, and to do all manner of iniquity; yea, in fine, all those who belong to the kingdom of the devil are they who need fear, and tremble, and quake; they are those who must be brought low in the dust; they are those who must be consumed as stubble" (1 Nephi 22:23). Moroni taught Joseph Smith that "they that come"—meaning the Lord and his destroying angels—"shall burn them, saith the Lord of

Hosts, that it shall leave them neither root nor branch" (Joseph Smith–History 1:37).

Thus the great day of division between the righteous and the wicked will come at the time of our Lord's second advent: "For the time speedily cometh that the Lord God shall cause a great division among the people, and the wicked will he destroy; and he will spare his people, yea, even if it so be that he must destroy the wicked by fire" (2 Nephi 30:10). Indeed, as a modern revelation attests, "at that hour cometh an entire separation of the righteous and the wicked; and in that day will I send mine angels to pluck out the wicked and cast them into unquenchable fire" (D&C 63:54).

That will be a day of power. Just as the power of the Almighty was felt in the cleansing of the earth in the days of Noah, wherein the earth received its baptism, so also will that same power be manifest in the last days when the earth is cleansed by fire and receives its "confirmation." "After you have been immersed," Elder Orson Pratt observed, "as this earth was, in the water, and been cleansed and received the remission of your sins, you also have the promise of baptism of fire and of the Holy Ghost, by which you are purified, as well justified and sanctified from all your evil affections, and you feel to love God and that which is just and true, and to hate that which is sinful and evil. Why? Because of this sanctifying, purifying principle that comes upon you, by the baptism of fire and the Holy Ghost. So must this earth be baptised by fire, it must be cleansed from all sin and impurity. Will it be filled with the Holy Ghost? Yes."[1]

A THIEF IN THE NIGHT

The scriptures speak of the Master returning as "a thief in the night" (1 Thessalonians 5:2; 2 Peter 3:10). It is true that no mortal man has known, does now know, or will yet know the precise day of the Lord's second advent. That is true for prophets and apostles as well as the rank and file of society and the Church. The Lord did not reveal to Joseph Smith the precise day and time of his coming (D&C 130:14–17). Elder M. Russell Ballard, speaking to students at Brigham Young University, observed: "I am called as one of the apostles to be a special witness of Christ in these exciting, trying times, and I do not know when He is going to come again. As far as I know, none of my brethren in the Council of the Twelve or even in the First Presidency know. And I would humbly suggest to you, my young brothers and sisters, that if we do not know, then *nobody* knows, no matter how compelling their arguments or how reasonable their calculations. . . . I believe when the Lord says 'no man' knows, it really means that no man knows. You should be extremely wary of anyone who claims to be an exception to divine decree."[2]

On the other hand, the Saints are promised that if they are in tune with the Spirit, they will recognize the season. The apostle Paul chose the descriptive analogy of a woman about to give birth. She may not know the exact hour or day when the child will be born, but one thing she knows for sure: *it will be soon*. It *must* be soon! The impressions and feelings and signs within her own body so testify. In that day, it may well be that the Saints of the Most High, the members of the body of Christ, will be pleading for the Lord to deliver the travailing earth, to bring an end to corruption and degradation, to introduce an era of peace and righteousness. And those who give heed to the words of scripture, especially to the living oracles (see D&C 68:10–11), will stand as the "children of light, and the children of the day," those who "are not of the night, nor of darkness" (1 Thessalonians 5:2–5). In a modern revelation the Savior declared: "And again, verily I say unto you, the coming of the Lord draweth nigh, and *it overta-keth the world as a thief in the night*—therefore, gird up your loins, that you may be the children of light, and that day shall not over-take you as a thief" (D&C 106:4–5; emphasis added).

As we move closer to the end of time, we would do well to live in such a manner that we can discern the signs of the times. We would be wise also to keep our eyes fixed and our ears riveted on those called to direct the destiny of this Church. The Prophet Joseph Smith pointed out that a particular man in his day who claimed prophetic powers "has not seen the sign of the son of man, as foretold by Jesus; neither has any man, nor will any man, till after the sun shall have been darkened and the moon bathed in blood, for the Lord hath not shown me any such sign, and, as the prophet saith, so it must be: *Surely the Lord God will do noth-ing, but he revealeth his secret unto his servants the prophets.* (See Amos 3:7)."[3]

THE WICKED ARE CONSUMED

When he comes in glory, all will know. "Wherefore, prepare ye for the coming of the Bridegroom; go ye, go ye out to meet him. For behold, he shall stand upon the mount of Olivet, and upon the mighty ocean, even the great deep, and upon the is-lands of the sea, and upon the land of Zion. And he shall utter his voice out of Zion, and he shall speak from Jerusalem, and *his voice shall be heard among all people;* and it shall be a voice as the voice of many waters, and as the voice of a great thunder, which shall break down the mountains, and the valleys shall not be found" (D&C 133:19–22; emphasis added).

The righteous dead from ages past—those who qualify for the first resurrection, specifically those who died true to the faith since the time the first resurrection began in the meridian of time—will come with the Savior when he returns in glory. The apostle Paul wrote: "I would not have you to be ignorant, brethren, concerning them which are asleep, that ye sorrow not, even as others which have no hope. For if we believe that Jesus died and rose again, even so them also which sleep in Jesus will God bring with him. For this we say unto you by the word of the Lord, that they who are alive at the coming of the Lord, shall not prevent [precede or be preferred before] them who remain unto the coming of the Lord, who are asleep. For the Lord himself shall descend from heaven with a shout, with the voice of the archangel, and with the trump of God; and the dead in Christ shall rise first; then they who are alive, shall be caught up together into the clouds with them who remain, to meet the Lord in the air; and so shall we be ever with the Lord" (JST, 1 Thessalonians 4:13–17).

Malachi prophesied that "the day cometh, that shall burn as an oven; and all the proud, yea, and all that do wickedly, shall be stubble: and the day that cometh shall burn them up, saith the Lord of hosts, that it shall leave them neither root nor branch" (Malachi 4:1; compare 2 Nephi 26:4; D&C 133:64). In 1823 Moroni quoted this passage differently to the seventeen-year-old Joseph Smith: "And all the proud, yea, and all that do wickedly shall burn as stubble; for *they that come* shall burn them, saith the Lord of Hosts" (Joseph Smith–History 1:37; emphasis added). In the Doctrine and Covenants the Lord of Justice declares: "For the hour is nigh and the day soon at hand when the earth is ripe; and all the proud and they that do wickedly shall be as stubble; and *I will burn them up*, saith the Lord of Hosts, that wickedness shall not be upon the earth" (D&C 29:9; emphasis added), "for after today cometh the burning," a day wherein "all the proud and they that do wickedly shall be as stubble; and *I will burn them up*, for I am the Lord of Hosts; and I will not spare any that remain in Babylon" (D&C 64:24; emphasis added).

The second coming of Christ in glory is a day in which "every corruptible thing, both of man, or of beasts of the field, or of the fowls of the heavens, or of the fish of the sea, that dwells upon all the face of the earth, shall be consumed; and also that of element shall melt with fervent heat; and all things shall become new, that my knowledge and glory may dwell upon all the earth" (D&C 101:24–25; compare 133:41; 2 Peter 3:10). President Joseph Fielding Smith wrote: "Somebody said, 'Brother Smith, do you mean to say that it is going to be literal fire?' I said, 'Oh, no, it will not be literal fire any more than it was literal water that covered the earth in the flood.'"[4]

The scriptures state that when the Savior appears he will be clothed in red. Red is symbolic of victory—victory over the devil, death, and hell. It is the symbol of salvation, of being placed beyond the power of all one's enemies.[5] Christ's red apparel will also symbolize both aspects of his ministry to fallen humanity—his mercy and his justice. Because he has trodden the wine-press alone, "even the wine-press of the fierceness of the wrath of Almighty God" (D&C 76:107; 88:106), he has descended below all things and mercifully taken upon him our stains, our blood, or our sins (2 Nephi 9:44; Jacob 1:19; 2:2; Alma 5:22). He comes in "dyed garments" as the God of justice, who has trampled the wicked beneath his feet: "And the Lord shall be red in his apparel, and his garments like him that treadeth in the winevat. And so great shall be the glory of his presence that the sun shall hide his face in shame, and the moon shall withhold its light, and the stars shall be hurled from their places. And his voice shall be heard: I have trodden the wine-press alone, and have brought judgment upon all people; and none were with me; and I have trampled them in my fury, and I did tread upon them in mine anger, and their blood have I sprinkled upon my garments, and stained all my raiment; for this was the day of vengeance which was in my heart" (Isaiah 63:1; D&C 133:48–51).

In his inimitable style, Elder Neal A. Maxwell observed: "Soon, . . . all flesh shall see Him together. All knees shall bow in His presence, and all tongues confess His name. Knees that never before assumed *that* posture for *that* purpose will do so then—and promptly. Tongues that never before have spoken His name except in gross profanity will do so then—and worshipfully.

"Soon, He who was once mockingly dressed in purple will come again, attired in red apparel, reminding us whose blood redeemed us. All will then acknowledge the completeness of His justice and His mercy and will see how human indifference to God—not God's indifference to humanity—accounts for so much misery and suffering. Then we will see the true story of mankind—and not through glass darkly. The great military battles will appear as mere bonfires that blazed briefly, and the mortal accounts of the human experience will be mere graffiti on the walls of time."[6]

THOSE WHO REMAIN

Those who are of at least a terrestrial level of righteousness will continue to live as mortals after the Lord returns. We are reminded in Doctrine and Covenants 76, the vision of the glories, that terrestrial beings are the good people of the earth, noble individuals who live according to the highest standards of virtue and decency and honor they know, but they are not valiant in the testimony of Jesus to such an extent that they seek for and receive the fulness of the everlasting gospel (D&C 76:71–80).

The Saints will live to "the age of man"—the age of one

hundred, according to Isaiah 65:20—and will then pass through death and be changed instantly from mortality to resurrected immortality: "Yea, and blessed are the dead that die in the Lord, . . . when the Lord shall come, and old things shall pass away, and all things become new, they shall rise from the dead and shall not die after, and shall receive an inheritance before the Lord, in the holy city. And he that liveth when the Lord shall come, and hath kept the faith, blessed is he; nevertheless, it is appointed to him to die at the age of man. Wherefore, children shall grow up until they become old"—that is, no longer will little ones die before the age of accountability; "old men shall die; but they shall not sleep in the dust, but they shall be changed in the twinkling of an eye" (D&C 63:49–51; see also JST, Isaiah 65:20).

Speaking of those mortals who remain on earth when the Lord comes in glory, President Joseph Fielding Smith pointed out that "the inhabitants of the earth will have a sort of translation. They will be transferred to a condition of the terrestrial order, and so they will have power over disease and they will have power to live until they get a certain age and then they will die."[7]

MAY WE HASTEN HIS COMING?

We hear once in a while the plea for us as Latter-day Saints to repent and improve so that we can hasten the Savior's second coming. It is true that we are under obligation to be faithful to our covenants, to deny ourselves of every worldly lust and cross ourselves as to the enticements of a decaying society, and to live as Saints. It is true that our labor is to build up the kingdom of God and establish Zion, all in preparation for the second coming of the Master. The full redemption of Zion depends on the urgency with which the Saints of the Most High pursue their sacred duty. Further, our righteous quest to be a light to a darkened world assures our own readiness to receive the Savior. But the time of his coming is a constant, not a variable. It may not be postponed because of the Saints' tardiness or sloth, any more than it can be hastened through a burst of goodness. But the Father knows when the King of Zion (Moses 7:53) will return to earth to preside over the kingdom of God. As was the case with his first coming to earth in the meridian of time, so it is in regard to his second coming. The Nephite prophets, for example, did not encourage the people to be faithful so that the Lord could come soon; rather, they stated forthrightly that in six hundred years he would come (see, for example, 1 Nephi 10:4; 19:8; 2 Nephi 25:19)—ready or not! Likewise, though we have not been told the day and the hour, that day and that hour are known. The time is set. It is fixed.[8] "The God of heaven has ordained that day," President Gordon B. Hinckley told us. "The prophets of all dispensations have spoken of it. We know not when it will come, but its dawning is certain."[9]

The early elders of the Church were instructed: "Wherefore, be of good cheer, and do not fear, for I the Lord am with you, and will stand by you; and ye shall bear record of me, even Jesus Christ, that I am the Son of the living God, that I was, that I am, and that I am to come" (D&C 68:6). Answer after answer after divine answer concerning such matters as the divine Sonship of Christ, his infinite and eternal atoning sacrifice, the principles of his eternal gospel—these things are made known with great power and persuasion. In addition, the revelations testify that—

- He will come again to reign among the Saints and to come down in judgment upon Idumea or the world (D&C 1:36);
- He will gather his faithful as a hen gathers her chicks and enable them to partake of the waters of life (D&C 10:64–66; 29:2; 33:6);

- Satan and the works of Babylon will be destroyed (D&C 1:16; 19:3; 35:11; 133:14);
- This dispensation of the gospel represents his last pruning of the vineyard (D&C 24:19; 33:2–3; 39:17; 43:28);
- The elect in the last days will hear his voice; they will not be asleep because they will be purified (D&C 35:20–21);
- We will have no laws but his laws when he comes; he will be our ruler (D&C 38:22; 41:4; 58:22);
- From the Lord's perspective, according to his reckoning, his coming is nigh (D&C 63:53); he comes tomorrow (D&C 64:24); he comes quickly, suddenly (D&C 33:18; 35:27; 36:8; 39:24; 41:4; 68:35). Let us prepare now for the coming of our King.

Chapter 4

A THOUSAND YEARS
OF PEACE AND GLORY

*I*t is easy in our busy and complex world to become ensnared by programs, points of view, and ways of life that have no lasting value, no everlasting import. We are eternal beings involved in a mortal experience, and one of the tasks of this estate is to see to it that we do not become preoccupied with the ephemeral, that which is wholly temporal and which will eventually pass away. We live in a day of wickedness and vengeance, an era in this world's temporal existence when Satan, the god of the ungodly, rages in the hearts of individuals everywhere. But we look upon the present distress with an eye of faith, with an eye to the future, with the certain assurance that one day soon God will bring an abrupt end to all unholiness and inaugurate an age of peace and happiness. In a not too distant day, the light of the great Millennium will dawn, and things will be very different on this earth.

Elder Neal A. Maxwell wrote of the thousand-year reign of the Redeemer: "That millenarian moment will not spring out of senates, will not be propelled by mortal proclamations, and will not be traceable to treaties. Rather, the King, Jesus Christ, will have first established His kingdom and His people, physically and spiritually, and He will then come and judge all societies accord-ing to His standards, not secular standards."[1] Or, as Elder Jeffrey R. Holland noted, "In that day the Word will come with power, and there will be incomparable power in his words. In those last days Christ's judgment will be the truth he speaks and an ac-knowledgment of that truth from all who hear him." In short, "In that millennial moment the Messiah will usher in the peace for which all the righteous have wished, worked, and waited."[2]

THE MILLENNIUM BEGINS

The second coming in glory of our Lord and Savior begins the Millennium. The Millennium does not begin when Christ comes to Adam-ondi-Ahman, when he appears at his temple in Independence, Missouri, or when he stands upon the Mount of Olives in the midst of Armageddon. The Millennium will not come because men and women on earth have become noble and good or because Christian charity will have spread across the globe and goodwill is the order of the day. The Millennium will not come because technological advancements and medical miracles will have extended human life or because peace trea-ties among warring nations will have soothed injured feelings and eased political tensions for a time.

Rather, the Millennium will be brought in by power, by the power of him who is the King of kings and Lord of lords. Satan will be bound by power, and the glory of the Millennium will be maintained by the righteousness of those who are permitted to live on earth (1 Nephi 22:15, 26).

At the beginning of the Millennium the earth and all things on it will be quickened, made alive, and transfigured—lifted spiritually to a higher plane for a season. The earth will be trans-formed from a telestial to a terrestrial glory, to that paradisiacal condition of which the scriptures and the prophets speak, that glorious condition that prevailed in Eden before the Fall (Articles of Faith 1:10). There will indeed be a new heaven and a new earth (Isaiah 65:17; Revelation 21:1).

When "the face of the Lord shall be unveiled," then, in that day, "the saints that are upon the earth, who are alive, shall be quickened and be caught up to meet him" (D&C 88:95–96). That quickening would seem to entail the accentuation of man's spiritual nature. Elder Orson Pratt explained that "all the inhabitants who are spared from this fire—those who are not proud, and who do not do wickedly, will be cleansed more fully and filled with the glory of God. A partial change will be wrought upon them"—a type of translation—"not a change to immortality, like that which all the Saints will undergo when they are changed in the twinkling of an eye, from mortality to immortality; but so great will be the change then wrought that the children who are born into the world will grow up without sin unto salvation [see D&C 45:58]. Why will this be so? Because *that fallen nature, introduced by the fall, and transferred from parents to children, from generation to generation, will be, in a measure, eradicated by this change.*"[3]

THE FIRST RESURRECTION

The first resurrection began with the resurrection of Jesus Christ in the meridian of time. All the prophets and those who gave heed to the words of the prophets, from the days of Adam to Christ—and, we presume, all those who never had an opportunity in mortality to receive the gospel but would have received it if they had been given the privilege (D&C 137:7–9)—came forth from the grave some time after the rise of the Savior to immortal glory (see Mosiah 15:21–25; Alma 40:20). We have no indication that there has been a wholesale resurrection of Saints since the resurrection of the Savior.

"There are some who feel," President Ezra Taft Benson pointed out, "that the resurrection is going on continually and has been since that time. That is not scripturally true, but we do know that it is possible for our Father to call from the graves those whom He needs to perform special missions and special service. For example, we know of at least three [Peter, James, and Moroni] who have been called up since the resurrection of the Master and since that first mass resurrection when the graves were opened and many of the Saints arose."[4]

When the Master returns in glory to take charge of affairs on this earth, with him will come a host of the righteous dead. The first resurrection will thereby resume. Those who have died true to the faith, those who were valiant in the testimony of Jesus, who have kept the celestial law, will return to earth with resurrected, immortal bodies. "They who have slept in their graves shall come forth, for their graves shall be opened; and they also shall be caught up to meet him in the midst of the pillar of heaven—they are Christ's, the first fruits, they who shall descend with him first, and they who are on the earth and in their graves, who are first caught up to meet him" (D&C 88:97–98). Or, according to the testimony of the apostle Paul, "they who are alive"—meaning, physically alive when the Lord comes—"shall be caught up together into the clouds with them who remain, to meet the Lord in the air; and so shall we be ever with the Lord" (JST, 1 Thessalonians 4:17). This is the first resurrection, or, as we have come to call it, the morning of the first resurrection, the resurrection of the celestial.

With Christ will come the hosts of persons who were translated before the resurrection of Christ, those who were taken into terrestrial glory without tasting death. Enoch and Melchizedek with their cities, Elijah and Moses and Alma and Nephi, and, surely, congregations and communities of the pure in heart of which we have no knowledge, will return as resurrected personages. These were with Christ in his resurrection (see D&C 133:54–55). Those who have been translated since the resurrection of Christ—John the Beloved, the three Nephites, and other holy men and women (D&C 49:8)—will undergo the change equivalent to death and be transformed instantaneously from their translated mortal state to resurrected immortality at the time of our Savior's return in glory (see 3 Nephi 28:8).[5]

A NEW KIND OF MORTALITY

Although persons who are alive at the time of Christ's second coming will be changed and quickened, they will yet continue to live as mortals. That is, for them death and immortality lie ahead. The mortal Saints will live to "the age of man" (D&C 63:50) during the Millennium; that age is one hundred years according to Isaiah (Isaiah 65:20). At that point they will pass from mortality through death into resurrected immortality instantly, "in the twinkling of an eye." For these persons there will be no time for the body in the grave, no sojourn in the postmortal world of spirits, for they will be received into glory immediately after their death: "Wherefore, children shall grow up until they become old; old men shall die; but they shall not sleep in the dust, but they shall be changed in the twinkling of an eye" (D&C 63:51).

Why it is that certain persons, perhaps billions of our brothers and sisters, will be sent to earth to gain their mortal and then immortal bodies during this glorious era—an era during which they will not be tested, at least in the same ways we are now—is not known. This we do know, however: our God is perfectly just. He is perfectly merciful. And he is impartial. He is no respecter of persons and delights in the development and ultimate salvation of all his sons and daughters. He is all-wise and all-knowing, and thus we would assume that he would arrange and orchestrate the times and seasons and events of our lives in such a way as to maximize our growth and further our spirituality. The Saints of the Most High ought to glory in the knowledge that so many could come to the earth and be born, nurtured in an Edenic atmosphere, and grow up without sin unto salvation (D&C 45:58).

When the telestial elements are stripped away from this orb, when sin and iniquity are burned away by the brightness of the coming of the King of Zion, the wickedness that befouls the planet will be no more and the earth will rest. No longer will Mother Earth cry out in painful weariness because of the pollutions upon her surface (Moses 7:48; compare Romans 8:22), for the stains of wilful sin will have been purged out, and the glory of heaven will be felt by every person. The Savior will be in our midst (3 Nephi 20:22; 21:25). He will reign over Zion and minister among his chosen people in both the Old and the New Jerusalem. He will dwell among his Saints, no doubt teach them in their congregations, and see to it that his doctrine is declared from one end of this earth to the other.

THE GREAT DAY OF GATHERING

As we discussed in *Living in the Eleventh Hour,* one of the grand signs of the times is that the fulness of the gospel of Jesus Christ will be preached to all the world. Not all, however, will have the privilege as mortals of receiving the gospel fulness, and not all will have that privilege before the Second Coming. The great day of gathering—the day when millions upon millions will come into the true fold of God—is millennial. But there is more.

Before the Lord Jesus returns in glory, the scriptures affirm that there will be kings and priests, queens and priestesses, in every nation, kindred, tongue, and people (Revelation 5:9–10). The revelations declare: "Prepare ye the way of the Lord, and make his paths straight, for the hour of his coming is nigh—When the Lamb shall stand upon Mount Zion, and with him a hundred and forty-four thousand, having his father's name written on their foreheads" (D&C 133:17–18). This group of 144,000 are high priests after the holy order of God, men who have themselves received the promise of exaltation and whose mission it is to bring as many as will come into the church of the Firstborn (see D&C 77:11), that inner circle of men and women who have passed the tests of mortality and have become the elect of God.[6] It may be that the 144,000 high priests called in the last days to bring people into the church of the Firstborn is a symbolic reference: In that day of division, of unspeakable wickedness and consummate righteousness, temples will dot the earth, be accessible to the Lord's covenant people everywhere, and thus the fulness of those temple blessings will be sealed upon millions of the faithful Saints worldwide by those holding those transcendent powers.

In the meridian of time, by command of the Savior, the gospel of Jesus Christ was delivered first to the Jews and later to the Gentiles. In our day, the gospel was delivered first to Joseph Smith and the Latter-day Saints, those of us who are "identified with the Gentiles" (D&C 109:60), that is, those who are Israelite by descent (see D&C 52:2; 86:8–10) and Gentile by culture. The gospel is given to us, and we bear the responsibility to take the message of the Restoration to the descendants of Lehi and to the Jews (1 Nephi 22:7–11). We therefore live in "the times of the Gentiles." "And when the times of the Gentiles is come in, a light shall break forth among them that sit in darkness, and it shall be the fulness of my gospel" (D&C 45:28). It is a time, in the words of President Marion G. Romney, in which "in this last dispensation, the gospel is to be preached primarily to the non-Jewish people of the earth."[7]

In a day yet future, at a time when the Gentiles—presumably those outside the Church as well as some from within the fold—sin against the fulness of the gospel and reject its supernal blessings, the Lord will take away these privileges from the Gentile nations and once again make them available primarily to his ancient covenant people (3 Nephi 16:10–11). This will be known as the fulfillment of the times of the Gentiles (1 Nephi 15:13) or the fulness of the "times of the Gentiles" (D&C 45:28). Because the people of the earth at that day refuse to receive the light of gospel fulness and turn their hearts from the Lord because of the precepts of men, "in that generation shall the times of the Gentiles be fulfilled" (D&C 45:29–30). In the purest sense, that will not take place until Jesus sets his foot upon Olivet and the Jews acknowledge their long-awaited Messiah.

As we know, there have been numerous legends, traditions, and a myriad of folktales dealing with the location and eventual return of the ten lost tribes, those from the northern part of Israel who were taken captive by the Assyrians in 721 B.C. During my youth in the Church, I heard a whole host of things: that the lost tribes were in the center of the earth, on a knob attached to the earth, on another planet, and so forth. Each of these traditions had its own source of authority. Since that time, and particularly since I discovered the doctrinal treasures within the Book of Mormon, I have concluded simply that the ten tribes are scattered among the nations, lost as much to their identity as to their whereabouts (1 Nephi 22:3–4). Thus the restoration, or gathering, of the ten tribes consists in scattered Israel—descendants of Jacob through such tribes as Reuben, Gad, Asher, Naphtali, Zebulun, and, of course, Joseph—coming to the knowledge of the restored gospel, accepting Christ's gospel (1 Nephi 15:14), coming into the true church and fold of God (2 Nephi 9:2), congregating with the faithful, and receiving the ordinances of the house of the Lord.[8] That is to say, the ten tribes will be gathered as all others are gathered—through conversion to the gospel of Jesus Christ.

We have witnessed miracles as the gospel has made its way into many parts of the earth, but the greatest miracles lie ahead. Leaning heavily upon the words of even more ancient prophets, Nephi recorded: "And the time cometh speedily that the righteous must be led up as calves of the stall, and *the Holy One of Israel must reign in dominion, and might, and power, and great glory. And he gathereth his children from the four quarters of the earth*; and he numbereth his sheep; and they know him; and there shall be one fold and one shepherd; and he shall feed his sheep, and in him they shall find pasture" (1 Nephi 22:24–25; emphasis added; see also 2 Nephi 30:6–18).

"Therefore, behold, the days come, saith the Lord, that it shall no more be said, The Lord liveth, that brought up the children of Israel out of the land of Egypt; but, The Lord liveth, that brought up the children of Israel from the land of the north, and from all the lands whither he had driven them: and I will bring them again into their land that I gave unto their fathers." And how is this great gathering to be accomplished? "Behold, I will send for many fishers, saith the Lord, and they shall fish them; and after will I send for many hunters, and they shall hunt them from every mountain, and from every hill, and out of the holes of the rocks. For mine eyes are upon all their ways" (Jeremiah 16:14–17).

The risen Lord explained to the Nephites that after his second coming, once he has begun to dwell on earth with his faithful, "then shall the work of the Father"—the work of the gathering of Israel—"commence at that day, even when this gospel shall be preached among the remnant of this people. Verily I say unto you, at that day shall the work of the Father commence among all the dispersed of my people, yea, even the tribes which have been lost, which the Father hath led out of Jerusalem" (3 Nephi 21:25–26). It will commence in the sense that it will be of such magnitude as to cause earlier efforts at gathering to pale in significance.

The return of the ten tribes is spoken of in modern revelation in majestic symbolism: "And the Lord, even the Savior, shall stand in the midst of his people, and shall reign over all flesh" (D&C 133:25). Further, those who are descendants of the northern tribes will respond to the gospel message, come under the direction of those prophets or priesthood leaders in their midst, traverse that highway we know as the "way of holiness" (Isaiah 35:8), and eventually participate in temple ordinances that make of us kings and queens, priests and priestesses, before God; they will "fall down and be crowned with glory, even in Zion, by the hands of the servants of the Lord, even the children of Ephraim," those who are entrusted with the keys of salvation (D&C 133:26–32).

"How long can rolling waters remain impure?" the Prophet Joseph Smith wrote by inspiration while in Liberty Jail. "What power shall stay the heavens? As well might man stretch forth his puny arm to stop the Missouri river in its decreed course, or to turn it up stream, as to hinder the Almighty from pouring down knowledge from heaven upon the heads of the Latter-day Saints" (D&C 121:33). The Saints have been blessed beyond measure with light and truth and sacred insights; the scriptures of the Restoration now shed forth their resplendent rays upon a darkened and benighted world. But there is more to come, more light, more knowledge, more doctrine, more precepts. Nothing is more set and established than the eternal fact that the canon of scripture is open and expanding.

We thrill in the assurance that other sacred volumes chronicling our Redeemer's ministry to the lost tribes shall come forth during the Millennium (2 Nephi 29:13). Elder Neal A. Maxwell made the following comment about additional scripture to be received in days yet to come: "Many more scriptural writings will yet come to us, including those of Enoch (see D&C 107:57), all the writings of the Apostle John (see Ether 4:16), the records of the lost tribes of Israel (2 Nephi 29:13), and the [remaining portion] of the Book of Mormon plates that were sealed. . . . Today we carry convenient quadruple combinations of the scriptures, but one day, since more scriptures are coming, we may need to pull little red wagons brimful with books."[9]

In November 1831 early elders of the Church were authorized to preach the gospel: "Go ye into the world, preach the gospel to every creature, acting in the authority which I have given you, baptizing in the name of the Father, and of the Son, and of the Holy Ghost" (D&C 68:8). "For, verily, the sound must go forth from this place into all the world, and unto the uttermost parts of the earth—the gospel must be preached unto every creature, with signs following them that believe" (D&C 58:64).

It is true that every person must have the opportunity to hear the gospel, either here or hereafter. Eventually "the truth of God will go forth boldly, nobly, and independent, till it has penetrated every continent, visited every clime, swept every country, and sounded in every ear, till the purposes of God shall be accomplished, and the Great Jehovah shall say the work is done."[10]

THE FINAL PHASE OF GATHERING

The work of gathering individuals into the fold of God is not complete when they are baptized and confirmed members of The Church of Jesus Christ of Latter-day Saints. The final phase of this divine process of gathering consists in gathering to holy temples to be endowed with power from on high and receiving therein the ordinances of exaltation.[11] It follows that because multitudes of souls will join themselves to the Saints in the Millennium, the work of temples will be among the most significant labor performed. "I think there is a work to be done [in the Millennium]," President Brigham Young said, "which the whole world seems determined we shall not do. What is it? To build temples."[12]

President Wilford Woodruff taught that "this work of administering the ordinances of the house of God to the dead . . . will require the whole of the Millennium, with Jesus at the head of the resurrected dead to attend to it."[13] President Joseph F. Smith likewise observed that "the great work of the Millennium shall be the work in the temples for the redemption of the dead; and then, we hope to enjoy the benefits of revelation through the Urim and Thummim, or by such means as the Lord may reveal concerning those for whom the work shall be done."[14] The scriptures attest that there will be kings and priests in every land and among every kindred, tongue, and people before the Lord Jesus comes in glory (Revelation 5:9–10). That implies, as we noted earlier, that temples will dot the earth, that the fulness of priesthood blessings will be available to individuals everywhere, even before the ushering in of the Millennium. Such sacred labor will be intensified during the thousand-year era of peace and righteousness, for "*to accomplish this work there will have to be not only one temple but thousands of them*, and thousands and tens of thousands of men and women will go into those temples and officiate for people who have lived as far back as the Lord shall reveal."[15]

NOT YET OF ONE FAITH

But not all who inhabit the earth during the beginning of the Millennium will be of one faith and one baptism. In that early hour of millennial splendor, not all will be converted to The Church of Jesus Christ of Latter-day Saints. Inasmuch as the terrestrial persons of the earth, those who are honorable and good, who are kindly and well disposed, will be spared the burning, they will live and move and have their being on the same earth as the members of the household of faith. Unfortunately, though, seeing is often not believing. Just as individuals are actuated and driven in this life by their quest for the fulness of truth, so also will individuals of a millennial kind be likewise driven and motivated. And just as noble and upright souls in all nations and climes hesitate in our day to partake of the glories of the new and everlasting covenant, so also will many decline the fulness of gospel light in that day when the Mediator of the new covenant presides among his Saints.

President Brigham Young stated: "If the Latter-day Saints think, when the kingdom of God is established on the earth, that all the inhabitants of the earth will join the church called Latter-day Saints, they are egregiously mistaken. I presume there will be as many sects and parties then as now."[16] On another occasion President Young said: "When Jesus comes to rule and reign as King of Nations as he now does King of Saints, the veil of the covering will be taken from all nations, that *all flesh may see his glory together, but that will not make them all Saints.* Seeing the Lord does not make a man a Saint, seeing an Angel does not make a man a Saint by any means." President Young then added that the leaders of nations in that day, "kings and potentates of the nations will come up to Zion to inquire after the ways of the Lord, and to seek out the great knowledge, wisdom, and understanding manifested through the Saints of the Most High. They will inform the people of God that they belong to such and such a Church, and do not wish to change their religion."[17] In short, "in the millennium men will have the privilege of being Presbyterians, Methodists, or Infidels, but they will not have the privilege of treating the name and character of Deity as they have done heretofore. No, but every knee shall bow and every tongue confess to the glory of God the Father that Jesus is the Christ."[18]

And yet the testimony of the scriptures and the prophets is consistent that as the power of God's Spirit continues to spread, eventually "the earth shall be full of the knowledge of the Lord, as the waters cover the sea" (Isaiah 11:9; see also Habakkuk 2:14). Truly "in that day when the Lord shall come, he shall reveal all things—things which have passed, and hidden things which no man knew, things of the earth, by which it was made, and the purpose and the end thereof—things most precious, things that are above, and things that are beneath, things that are in the earth, and upon the earth, and in heaven" (D&C 101:32–34).

"The gospel will be taught," President Joseph Fielding Smith observed, "far more intensely and with greater power during the millennium, *until all the inhabitants of the earth shall embrace it. . . .* Through the revelations given to the prophets, we learn that during the reign of Jesus Christ for a thousand years *eventually all people will embrace the truth.*"[19]

The Prophet Joseph Smith, drawing upon the prophecies of Zechariah 14:16–18, said, "There will be wicked men on the earth during the thousand years." By *wicked* he presumably meant those of a terrestrial order, those who refused to come unto the Father through receiving the fulness of his gospel (see D&C 84:48–53; see also 35:12).[20] The Prophet's statement continues: "The heathen nations who will not come up to worship will be visited with the judgments of God, and must eventually be destroyed from the earth" (see Isaiah 60:12).[21]

Likewise, Isaiah testified: "In those days there shall be no more thence an infant of days, nor an old man that hath not filled his days; for the child shall not die, but shall live to be an hundred years old; but *the sinner, living to be an hundred years old, shall be accursed*" (JST, Isaiah 65:20; emphasis added).

A SANCTIFIED SOCIALITY

We can only imagine such an existence—a life without physical pain, without premature death, without the sorrow that accompanies sin and waywardness, without the disappointment associated with dishonesty and greed. Isaiah proclaimed that in that day "the wolf also shall dwell with the lamb, and the leopard shall lie down with the kid; and the calf and the young lion and the fatling together; and a little child shall lead them. And the cow and the bear shall feed; their little ones shall lie down together: and the lion shall eat straw like the ox. And the sucking child shall play on the hole of the asp, and the weaned child shall put his hand on the cockatrice's den. They shall not hurt nor destroy in all my holy mountain" (Isaiah 11:6–9; compare 65:25). That is, "in that day the enmity of man, and the enmity of beasts, yea, the enmity of all flesh"—an animosity, a natural tension and unrest that came as a result of the Fall—"shall cease from before my face" (D&C 101:26). And so it is that "violence shall no more be heard in thy land, wasting nor destruction within thy borders; but thou shalt call thy walls Salvation, and thy gates Praise" (Isaiah 60:18).

Mortals will inhabit the earth alongside immortals during the entirety of the thousand years. Persons who abide the day of the Lord's coming in glory will continue to live on this earth in an Edenic state. They will labor and study and grow and interact and love and socialize as before, but such things will be undertaken in a totally moral environment. "When the Savior shall appear," the Prophet Joseph Smith taught in Nauvoo, "we shall see him as he is. We shall see that he is a man like ourselves. And *that same sociality which exists among us here will exist among us there, only it will be coupled with eternal glory, which glory we do not now enjoy*" (D&C 130:1–2; emphasis added). "And they shall build houses, and inhabit them; and they shall plant vineyards, and eat the fruit of them. They shall not build, and another inhabit; they shall not plant, and another eat" (Isaiah 65:21–22).

That is to say, in the Millennium individuals will enjoy the fruits of their labors. In a world where there is no extortion, no bribery, no organized crime, where there are no unjust laws, no class distinctions according to income or chances for learning, people will no longer be preyed upon by the perverse or the malicious through financial demands or pressures. Our longings for stability, for longevity, and for permanence will be largely satisfied, for the father of lies and those who have spread his influence will have no place on the earth during the thousand years.

"Now, how will it be on this earth when Christ reigns?" President George Q. Cannon inquired. "When the Millennium dawns," he answered his own question, "Satan bound and the elements of the earth at our disposal and under our control, there will be no hunger, no thirst, no nakedness, no vagrants, no houseless people; *all will have that which is necessary to supply their physical wants. But there will be no waste.* One man will not be allowed to lord it over another and take possession of more than he needs; but *all will have a fulness,* Satan will be bound. He will not have power to inflict the misery he has done and is doing."[22]

We suppose that the work of the Church and kingdom of God—the establishment of men, women, and children in eternal family units through the power of the Holy Priesthood—will come to complete fruition by the end of the Millennium. When, by the end of the thousand years, people of the Church will have achieved a unity of the faith, the Church of Jesus Christ, as we know it now, will have served its function (see Ephesians 4:11–14). What kind of a church, what ecclesiastical system of organization, will exist in eternity, beyond the patriarchal order, the order of the family, has not been made known.

The Millennium will be a time when so many of mortality's wrongs will be righted, when time's inequities will be eternally rectified. For example, as Elder Dallin H. Oaks taught, "We know that many wonderful and worthy Latter-day Saints currently lack the ideal opportunities and essential requirements for their progress. Singleness, childlessness, death, and divorce frustrate ideals and postpone the fulfillment of promised blessings. In addition, some women who desire to be full-time mothers and homemakers have been literally compelled to enter the full-time work force. But these frustrations are only temporary. The Lord has promised that in the eternities no blessing will be denied His sons and daughters who keep the commandments, are true to their covenants, and desire what is right.

"Many of the most important deprivations of mortality will be set right in the Millennium, which is the time for fulfilling all that is incomplete in the great plan of happiness for all of our Father's worthy children. We know that will be true of temple ordinances. *I believe it will also be true of family relationships and experiences.*"[23]

"One of the challenges of the faithful," Elder Jeffrey R. Holland observed, "is to realize that sometimes those who are not obedient and worthy seem to receive as many or more of the temporal blessings of life as do those who sacrifice and serve. . . . The Saints are to be faithful to the end without too many side-long glances at their neighbors. They are to keep the commandments because they are called to do so and because they need to be kept, regardless of the response of others." He added that "the faith and devotion of the faithful is recorded in the Lamb's book of life, and the day will come when they will be included among God's jewels. In that day it will matter very much who was righteous and who was wicked, who served God and who did not. In the meantime, all must remember that God does not settle his end-of-the-year accounts in September."[24]

We sing an anthem of praise and anticipation, a hymn that points our minds toward the glorious days ahead:

> *The day dawn is breaking, the world is awaking,*
> *The clouds of night's darkness are fleeing away.*
> *The worldwide commotion, from ocean to ocean,*
> *Now heralds the time of the beautiful day.*
>
> *In many a temple the Saints will assemble*
> *And labor as saviors of dear ones away.*
> *Then happy reunion and sweetest communion*
> *We'll have with our friends in the beautiful day.*
>
> *Still let us be doing, our lessons reviewing,*
> *Which God has revealed for our walk in his way;*

And then, wondrous story, the Lord in his glory
Will come in his pow'r in the beautiful day.

Beautiful day of peace and rest,
Bright be thy dawn from east to west.
Hail to thine earliest welcome ray,
Beautiful, bright, millennial day.[25]

Our Lord and God will govern his people from two world capitals, "for out of Zion shall go forth the law, and the word of the Lord from Jerusalem" (Isaiah 2:3). "And he shall utter his voice out of Zion"—meaning Independence, Missouri—"and he shall speak from Jerusalem, and his voice shall be heard among all people; and it shall be a voice as the voice of many waters, and as the voice of a great thunder, which shall break down the mountains, and the valleys shall not be found" (D&C 133:21–22). In that day the latter-day David, even Jesus Christ, the true son of David, will unite Ephraim and Judah and preside over all Israel, from one end of the earth to the other. Thus will be fulfilled the divine decree: "Be subject to the powers that be, until he reigns whose right it is to reign, and subdues all enemies under his feet" (D&C 58:22).

The apostle Paul taught that "in the dispensation of the fulness of times [the Lord would] gather together in one all things in Christ, both which are in heaven, and which are on earth; even in him" (Ephesians 1:10). And surely what begins as a flowing stream in our day will become a mighty river during the thousand years of peace. In that day the heavens will be opened, pure and sweet communion with God and angels will be enjoyed by the Saints of the Most High, and eternal truths will be made known constantly, without let or hindrance. The Saints will have been cleansed of sin, and their motives will have been purified; they will no longer ask amiss for that which they ought not. Thus, "in that day whatsoever any man shall ask, it shall be given unto him" (D&C 101:27). "And it shall come to pass, that before they call, I will answer; and while they are yet speaking, I will hear" (Isaiah 65:24).

During the thousand years, the covenant people of Christ's church on earth will have internalized the principles of his gospel and incorporated the law of the Lord into their very being. They will then see "eye to eye" with one another and with their Lord and Master (D&C 84:98). Jeremiah recorded the words of Jehovah: "Behold, the days come, saith the Lord, that I will make a new covenant with the house of Israel, and with the house of Judah: not according to the covenant that I made with their fathers in the day that I took them by the hand to bring them out of the land of Egypt; which my covenant they brake, although I was an husband unto them, saith the Lord: but this shall be the covenant that I will make with the house of Israel; after those days, saith the Lord, *I will put my law in their inward parts, and write it in their hearts*; and will be their God, and they shall be my people" (Jeremiah 31:31–33; emphasis added).

The people who have accepted the fulness of the gospel in that day will know their God and be constrained to obey his will and keep his commandments. "And they shall teach no more every man his neighbour, and every man his brother, saying, Know the Lord: for *they shall all know me*, from the least of them unto the greatest of them, saith the Lord: for I will forgive their iniquity, and I will remember their sin no more" (Jeremiah 31:34; emphasis added).

"How is this to be done?" Joseph Smith asked. "It is to be done by this sealing power, and the other Comforter"—the

Second Comforter, the Lord Jesus himself—"spoken of, which will be manifest by revelation."[26]

The millennial day will be a day when Christ and the resurrected Saints will dwell on earth—not permanently but periodically, "when they please, or when it is necessary to govern it."[27] It will be a time in which individuals will have grown up in the Lord (Helaman 3:21), will have cultivated the gifts of the Spirit, and will have received a fulness of the Holy Ghost (D&C 109:15). The Holy Ghost will have taught and sanctified them until they are prepared to come into the presence of Christ and even unto the Father.[28] It will be the day of the Second Comforter, the day when the Saints whose eyes are single to the glory of God will see him (D&C 88:67–68).

SATAN IS LOOSED

For a thousand years persons on earth will live lives of quiet nobility and will bow the knee to acknowledge Jesus the Messiah as the King of Zion and the Redeemer of all humankind. As we have noted, at the beginning of the Millennium not all of earth's inhabitants will join the true church, but by the end of the thousand years, all will be of one faith. Though Satan will have been dismissed from the earth by the true King of kings, and though he will have been bound by the righteousness of the people, persons will nonetheless have their moral agency. They will exercise the power of choice. For reasons that have not been fully revealed, there will come a time at the end of the thousand years when "men again begin to deny their God" (D&C 29:22), when the devil will be loosed for a "little season" (D&C 29:22; 43:31; 88:111; Revelation 20:7–8). That is, individuals will choose, despite the light and the truth that surround them, to come out in open rebellion against our Father, his Beloved Son, and the great plan of happiness. Satan will be loosed again "for a little season" that he might "gather together his armies" (D&C 88:111; see also 43:31).

Perhaps we can gain some insight into why such a turn of events will take place by searching the Book of Mormon. We remember during the almost two hundred years after the risen Lord's visit to America that all were converted to Christ, dealt justly with one another, had all things in common, and were united in that order of priesthood society we know as Zion. "And it came to pass that there was no contention in the land, because of the love of God which did dwell in the hearts of the people" (4 Nephi 1:15; see also vv. 1–17).

What changed things? It was *pride*, pride in what one was called, pride in what one earned, pride in one's dress and appearance, pride in one's place and station in society. "And from that time forth they did have their goods and their substance no more common among them. And they began to be divided into classes; and they began to build up churches unto themselves to get gain, and began to deny the true church of Christ" (4 Nephi 1:25–26; see also vv. 20–24).

President George Q. Cannon taught: "After the thousand years [Satan] will regain some of his present power. It will be as it was among the Nephites. . . . Men will arise who will object to working for the benefit of others; class distinctions will once more make themselves apparent."[29] On another occasion he explained that "when Satan is loosed again for a little while, when the thousand years shall be ended, it will be through mankind departing from the practice of those principles which God has revealed, and this Order of Enoch probably among the rest. He can, in no better way, obtain power over the hearts of the children of men, than by appealing to their cupidity, avarice, and low, selfish desires."[30]

It should be obvious that Satan's final conquest over the souls of men at the end of the Millennium will be limited to mortals. Exalted, immortal beings—those who have been changed in the twinkling of an eye, or resurrected personages who minister on earth from time to time—cannot fall, cannot apostatize. Their salvation is secure. The father of lies will thus have his way only among those living in mortality during the final years of the Millennium, those who have not arrived at the age of one hundred years. "When the period called the Millennium has passed away," Elder Orson Pratt explained, "Satan will again be loosed. Now the query arises, Will Satan have power to deceive those who have lived on the earth, and have fallen asleep for a moment, and have received their immortal bodies? No, he will not. When they have passed through their probation, and have received their immortal bodies, Satan will have no power over them. Thus generation after generation will pass away, during the Millennium, but by and by, at the close of that period, unnumbered numbers of the posterity of those who lived during the Millennium will be scattered in the four quarters of the earth, and Satan will be loosed, and will go forth and tempt them, and overcome some of them, so that they will rebel against God; not rebel in ignorance or dwindle in unbelief, as the Lamanites did; but they will sin willfully against the law of heaven."[31]

Those who choose to reject the Lord and his plan at that late date do so against the light of heaven; they in essence say that the sun does not shine while they see it. They are thus consigned hereafter to a kingdom of no glory as sons of perdition.[32] "Michael, the seventh angel, even the archangel, shall gather together his armies, even the hosts of heaven. And the devil shall gather together his armies; even the hosts of hell, and shall come up to battle against Michael and his armies. And then cometh the battle of the great God"—known also as the battle of Gog and Magog[33]—"and the devil and his armies shall be cast away into their own place, that they shall not have power over the saints any more at all" (D&C 88:112–14).

THE END OF THE EARTH

At the end of the thousand years, after the battle of Gog and Magog, we come to that time known as "the end of the earth" (D&C 88:101; Joseph Smith–Matthew 1:55), the final cleansing and celestialization of the planet. Having been baptized by water in the days of Noah and baptized by fire, or confirmed, at the time of the Second Coming, the earth will pass through the equivalent of a death and resurrection. It will become a glorified celestial orb, inasmuch as it will have filled the measure of its creation (D&C 88:25). The earth will then be a fit abode for the true and faithful, "that bodies who are of the celestial kingdom may possess it forever and ever; for, for this intent was it made and created, and for this intent are they sanctified" (D&C 88:20).

Those who seek to prepare themselves for what lies ahead, who have taken the Holy Spirit for their guide, attempt to view things as they are now in terms of things as they will be. One day things will change. Goodness and honesty and integrity will be the order of the day; morality and decency will characterize persons across the globe. If only for that reason, we look forward to the great millennial day. Though there are many tight places through which the Saints will be required to pass, though trials and difficulties will abound on every side, though disease and death and despair will be rampant prior to the Lord's coming, yet we glory in the fact that one day the King of kings and Lord of lords will take control of things, and a new day will dawn.

"For I, the Almighty, have laid my hands upon the nations, to scourge them for their wickedness. And plagues shall go forth, and they shall not be taken from the earth until I have completed my work, which shall be cut short in righteousness—until all shall know me, who remain, even from the least unto the greatest, and shall be filled with the knowledge of the Lord, and shall see eye to eye, and shall lift up their voice, and with the voice together sing this new song, saying:

> The Lord hath brought again Zion;
> The Lord hath redeemed his people, Israel,
> According to the election of grace,
> Which was brought to pass by the faith
> And covenant of their fathers.
> The Lord hath redeemed his people;
> And Satan is bound and time is no longer.
> The Lord hath gathered all things in one.
> The Lord hath brought down Zion from above.
> The Lord hath brought up Zion from beneath.
> The earth hath travailed and brought forth her strength;
> And truth is established in her bowels;
> And the heavens have smiled upon her;
> And she is clothed with the glory of her God;
> For he stands in the midst of his people.
> Glory, and honor, and power, and might,
> Be ascribed to our God; for he is full of mercy,
> Justice, grace and truth, and peace,
> Forever and ever, Amen.
> (D&C 84:96–102)

"And again, verily I say unto you, the coming of the Lord draweth nigh, and it overtaketh the world as a thief in the night—therefore, gird up your loins, that you may be the children of light, and that day shall not overtake you as a thief" (D&C 106:4–5). The faithful will not be surprised. The children of light, those who honor their covenants and are true to their trust, who seek for and cultivate the spirit of revelation, these shall be in a position to read the signs of the times and be prepared for the great and terrible day of the Lord. They will abide the day, be caught up to meet their Master, and feel peace and confidence in his presence.

Chapter 5

BEING RAISED FROM THE DEAD

$\mathcal{S}$ome time ago one of our daughters went through a difficult time of serious illness. For some reason, I found myself worrying and fretting to a degree I now acknowledge was disproportionate to the situation at the time. She was quite sick, but there was nothing to suggest that her life was in jeopardy. And yet I found myself thinking the worst—wondering what would happen to her family, how her husband would get by, and how her children would survive without their mom. But that was not the deepest anguish nor the most poignant fear. I found myself, for some strange reason, reflecting deeply on such morbid questions as the following: What if there is no life after death? What if this life is all there is? What if when we die we simply cease to exist? What if in fact we would never see her again after we laid her in the grave? The pain, the sorrow, the gloom and bitterness, the darkness that shrouded my soul are almost impossible to describe now; all I can say is that for a period of moments I found myself where I had never been before: in a mood of absolute existential despair, drowning in doubt and consumed by the pain of eternal separation. I wept and shuddered, shook my head and cried out, "No, no, it can't be!"

And then, as quickly as those evil and empty thoughts had entered onto the stage of my mind, they left. The Spirit of God was poured out upon me, and I felt the reassuring peace that passes all understanding, the tender assurance that God lives, and that he is in his heaven; that the plan of salvation is in very deed the great plan of happiness; that Jesus had in fact burst the bands of death and led captivity captive; that his rise from the tomb certified that we too will come forth from the grave in glory; and that life and love and learning are forever. Oh, the unspeakable relief I felt! It was as though the lights had been switched on and the darkness had been dispelled.

As I sat pondering on what had just taken place, my mind and heart were overrun with thoughts and feelings: I poured out my heart in gratitude to my Heavenly Father for the spiritual study in contrast I had just experienced. I thanked God for the testimony of Jesus that had been planted in my heart some six decades before. I praised him for allowing me to sense, for a brief moment in time, just how gloomy and helpless so many of earth's inhabitants feel when a loved one departs this life or when they themselves look into the eyes of the grim reaper. I grieved for a time with all those in the world who sorrow in the face of death without hope of deliverance or a firm knowledge of the immortality of the soul. As I contemplate that sobering experience, I am again overwhelmed with feelings of gratitude and love for the Father and the Son, for their love and tender mercies.

UNDERSTOOD BY THE ANCIENTS

Through the Prophet Joseph Smith's inspired translation of the Bible, we learn of the ministry of Enoch, that ancient prophet who has been such an enigma to both Jews and Christians. In writing about what had taken place some three millennia before the birth of Christ, Moses recorded: "And the Lord said unto Enoch: Look, and he looked and beheld the Son of Man lifted up on the cross, after the manner of men: and he heard a loud voice; and the heavens were veiled; and all the creations of God mourned; and the earth groaned; and the rocks were rent; and the saints arose, and were crowned at the right hand of the Son of Man, with crowns of glory; and as many of the spirits as were in prison came forth, and stood on the right hand of God; and the remainder were reserved in chains of darkness until the judgment of the great day" (Moses 7:55–57). This significant scriptural passage attests that the knowledge of life after death, the sweet assurance of the immortality of the soul, was had in earth's earliest ages.

More than a thousand years later, Abraham inquired concerning how, according to divine promise, he and his posterity would be given a land inheritance. "And Abram said, Lord God, how wilt thou give me this land for an everlasting inheritance? And the Lord said, *Though thou wast dead, yet am I not able to give it thee? And if thou shalt die, yet thou shalt possess it,* for the day cometh, that *the Son of man shall live; but how can he live if he be not dead? He must first be quickened.* And it came to pass that Abram looked forth and saw the days of the Son of Man, and was glad, and his soul found rest, and he believed in the Lord; and the Lord counted it unto him for righteousness" (JST, Genesis 15:9–12; emphasis added; see John 8:56; Helaman 8:17).

More than a thousand years after that, Isaiah recorded: "Thy dead men shall live, together with my dead body shall they arise. Awake and sing, ye that dwell in dust: for thy dew is as the dew of herbs, and the earth shall cast out the dead" (Isaiah 26:19). More than a century later, Ezekiel saw a vision of dry bones come together and form themselves into a human body, attesting not only that Israel would one day be united and become whole but also that mortals were destined to be raised from the grave by the power of God (Ezekiel 37). Job had asked the question of the ages: "If a man die, shall he live again?" (Job 14:14). He later answered his own question: "Oh that my words were now written! Oh that they were printed in a book! That they were graven with an iron pen and lead in the rock for ever! For I know that my Redeemer liveth, and that he shall stand at the latter day upon the earth: and though after my skin worms destroy this body, yet in my flesh shall I see God: whom I shall see for myself, and mine eyes shall behold, and not another; though my reins be consumed within me" (Job 19:23–27).

When Jesus Christ ministered among the people and spoke of the resurrection, few understood his strange teaching. No one had ever risen from the dead. There was no precedent. There was nothing to compare it to. How could mortals, who were well acquainted with aging and pain and bodily decay, grasp this doctrine of doctrines, this mystery of salvation? Simon Peter had spent three years beside his Master, traveling from village to village, gazing with awe as Jesus ministered to the widows, healed the children of Roman officials, taught the gospel of the kingdom, exposed and condemned the hypocrisy and self-righteousness of his enemies, and sought to prepare his chosen Twelve for his eventual departure. Peter had been privy to sacred moments, had witnessed firsthand the mercy and majesty of this most unusual but powerful man, this Jesus of Nazareth. He had, in private quarters, seen the dead brought back to life. He had, in the midst of multitudes, beheld the lowly Nazarene feed five thousand men, plus women and children, with only five loaves of bread and two fishes.

Simon Peter had, on the holy mount, been transfigured, lifted spiritually to a higher plane, with his Lord and his apostolic associates James and John; had heard the voice of God the Father speak out of the Shekinah, the holy cloud; and had received the more sure word of prophecy and thereby gained the assurance of eternal life (2 Peter 1:19; D&C 131:5–6).[1] He had witnessed the arrest of Jesus, had beheld at least a part of the mock trials, and had seen his world come crashing down as the Messiah yielded himself into the hands of sinful men and to the ignominy of death by crucifixion. Peter's was a cold, dark, and dreary world for three days, as the Jews counted time.

But the morning of resurrection came. Reports reached the senior apostle that the tomb was empty, that Christ had burst the bands of death, that Jesus had risen from the grave. Eventually Peter was blessed with a personal appearance of the risen Lord and met with Jesus in company with the other apostles on several occasions. Peter was delighted but mystified, excited but confused, thrilled but filled with questions. What did it all mean?

The apostle Paul taught that "if in this life only we have hope in Christ, we are of all men most miserable" (1 Corinthians 15:19). If Jesus' greatest accomplishments consisted of his kindness, his generosity, and his sage advice, then our hope for happiness hereafter is unfounded. Like Paul, the Book of Mormon prophet Jacob declared that if Christ did not rise from the dead (as it was prophesied that he would do), then we would, one and all, at the time of death be consigned to spiritual ruin and destruction; we would be forevermore subject to the father of lies. Why? Because if Jesus did not have the power to rise from the dead and thus redeem the body from the grave, then he surely did not have the power to forgive sins and thereby redeem the spirit from hell (2 Nephi 9:7–9; compare 1 Corinthians 15:12–17). "If the resurrection from the dead be not an important point, or item in our faith," the Prophet Joseph Smith explained, "we must confess that we know nothing about it; for if there be no resurrection from the dead, then Christ has not risen; and if Christ has not risen He was not the Son of God." On the other hand, "if He has risen from the dead the bands of the temporal death are broken that the grave has no victory. If, then, the grave has no victory, those who keep the sayings of Jesus and obey His teachings have not only a promise of a resurrection from the dead, but an assurance of being admitted into His glorious kingdom."[2] Because Jesus Christ has risen from the dead, we also will rise from the dead. Because he lives, we will live also, beyond the grave (1 Corinthians 15:21–22; Alma 11:40–41).

THE BODY RESTORED, THE IDENTITY RETAINED

The resurrected body is a spiritual body, meaning that it is immortal, not subject to death (1 Corinthians 15:44; Alma 11:45; D&C 88:27). The scriptural promise is that we come forth from the grave with a resurrected body suited to the respective kingdom we will inherit: "They who are of a celestial spirit shall receive the same body which was a natural body; even ye shall receive your bodies, and your glory shall be that glory by which your bodies are quickened. Ye who are quickened by a portion of the celestial glory [in this life] shall then [in the resurrection] receive of the same, even a fulness. And they who are quickened by a portion of the terrestrial glory shall then receive of the same, even a fulness. And also they who are quickened by a portion of the telestial glory shall then receive of the same, even a fulness. And they who remain [the sons of perdition] shall also be quickened; nevertheless, they shall return again to their own place, to enjoy that which they are willing to receive, because they were not willing to enjoy that which they might have received" (D&C 88:28–32).

The scriptures of the Restoration clarify the nature of the resurrected body. "The soul [meaning, in this instance, the spirit] shall be restored to the body," Alma explained, "and the body to the soul; yea, and every limb and joint shall be restored to its body; yea, even a hair of the head shall not be lost; but all things shall be restored to their proper and perfect frame" (Alma 40:23; see also 11:43). In speaking of the righteous who waited anxiously for the Savior's entrance into paradise, President Joseph F. Smith declared: "Their sleeping dust was to be restored unto its perfect frame, bone to his bone, and the sinews and the flesh upon them, the spirit and the body to be united never again to be divided, that they might receive a fulness of joy" (D&C 138:17). Latter-day prophets have instructed that the body comes forth from the grave as it is laid down, "whether old or young; there will not be 'added unto their stature one cubit,' neither taken from it; all will be raised by the power of God, having spirit in their bodies, and not blood."[3] We are not to understand from this statement that physical deformities will be a part of the resurrected body, for "deformity will be removed; defects will be eliminated, and men and women shall attain to the perfection of their spirits, to the perfection that God designed in the beginning."[4]

On one occasion Elder Orson Pratt pointed out that a person's mortal body is constantly changing as old cells are replaced by new ones, and so forth. The Prophet Joseph taught: "There is no fundamental principle belonging to a human system that ever goes into another in this world or in the world to come; I care not what the theories of men are. We have the testimony that God will raise us up, and he has the power to do it. If any one supposes that any part of our bodies, that is, the fundamental parts thereof, ever goes into another body, he is mistaken."[5] President Brigham Young, who was tutored by that choice seer, Joseph Smith, said: "The question may be asked, do not the particles that compose man's body, when returned to mother earth, go to make or compose other bodies? No, they do not [see D&C 88:28]. . . . Neither can the particles which have comprised the body of man become parts of the bodies of other men, or of beasts, fowls, fish, insect, or vegetables. They are governed by divine law and though they may pass from the knowledge of the scientific world, that divine law still holds, governs and controls them. Man's body may be buried in the ocean, it may be eaten by wild beasts, or it may be burned to ashes, they may be scattered to the four winds, yet the particles of which it is composed will not be incorporated into any form of vegetable or animal life, to become a component part of their structure. . . . At the sound of the trumpet of God every particle of our physical structures necessary to make our tabernacles perfect will be assembled, to be rejoined with the spirit, every man in his order. Not one particle will be lost."[6]

Hence, "the spirit and the body are the soul of man. And the resurrection from the dead is the redemption of the soul" (D&C 88:15–16; compare Mormon 9:13–14).

We have the comforting assurance that even though we will be refined, renewed, and perfected body and soul in the resurrection, we will maintain our identity. We will know friends and loved ones in and after the resurrection, even as we know them now. Though some Christians at the time of Joseph Smith (and many today) spoke of being caught up into the love of Jesus and blending into his nature, the revelations of heaven declared otherwise. In speaking of meeting a departed loved one in the future, President Joseph F. Smith taught: "I expect to be able to recognize her, just as I could recognize her tomorrow, if she were living. . . . because her identity is fixed and indestructable, just as fixed and indestructable as the identity of God the Father and Jesus Christ the Son. They cannot be any other than themselves. They cannot be changed; they are from everlasting to everlasting, eternally the same; so it will be with us. We will progress and develop and grow in wisdom and understanding, but our identity can never change."[7]

RESURRECTION AND JUDGMENT

In the Book of Mormon, resurrection and eternal judgment are companion doctrines, just as are the Fall and the Atonement. One of the great acts of mercy and grace is that all individuals who took a physical body, including the sons of perdition, will be resurrected and thereafter brought to stand before God to be judged of their works. In a sense, therefore, the Atonement overcomes spiritual death for all, at least for the short season in which all will stand once again in the divine presence.

Jacob wrote: "And it shall come to pass that when all men shall have passed from this first death unto life, insomuch as they have become immortal, they must appear before the judgment-seat of the Holy One of Israel; and then cometh the judgment, and then must they be judged according to the holy judgment of God" (2 Nephi 9:15). Samuel the Lamanite also declared that Jesus "surely must die that salvation may come; yea, it behooveth him and becometh expedient that he dieth, to bring to pass the resurrection of the dead, that thereby men may be brought into the presence of the Lord" (Helaman 14:15; compare 3 Nephi 27:13–16). Moroni too bore witness that "because of Jesus Christ came the redemption of man. And because of the redemption of man, which came by Jesus Christ, they are brought back into the presence of the Lord; yea, *this is wherein all men are redeemed*" (Mormon 9:12–13; emphasis added).

Jesus taught that "the Father judgeth no man, but hath committed all judgment unto the Son" (John 5:22). Similarly, Jacob, son of Lehi, beckoned to his people: "O then, my beloved brethren, come unto the Lord, the Holy One. Remember that his paths are righteous. Behold, the way for man is narrow, but it lieth in a straight course before him, and *the keeper of the gate is the Holy One of Israel; and he employeth no servant there*; and there is none other way save it be by the gate; for he cannot be deceived, for the Lord God is his name" (2 Nephi 9:41; emphasis added).

But is it not the case that every single person who has lived on earth must stand before God to be judged? Did not John the Revelator describe that poignant moment? "And I saw the dead, small and great, stand before God; and the books were opened: and another book was opened, which is the book of life: and the dead were judged out of those things which were written in the books, according to their works" (Revelation 20:12). In a modern revelation, the Savior explained that "mine apostles, the Twelve which were with me in my ministry at Jerusalem, shall stand at my right hand at the day of my coming in a pillar of fire, be-ing clothed with robes of righteousness, with crowns upon their heads, in glory even as I am, to judge the whole house of Israel, *even as many as have loved me and kept my commandments, and none else*" (D&C 29:12; emphasis added).

Thus Elder Bruce R. McConkie offered this thought: "Christ's judicial decisions are those of the other two members of the Godhead because all three are perfectly united as one. The an-cient Twelve and the Nephite Twelve, *and no doubt others similarly empowered, will sit in judgment, under Christ,* on selected portions of the house of Israel."[8] Elsewhere Elder McConkie pointed out: "The reality is that *there will be a whole hierarchy of judges* who, under Christ, shall judge the righteous. He alone shall issue the decrees of damnation for the wicked."[9]

A HOLY ORDINANCE

The early leaders of this dispensation taught that resurrection was an ordinance that must be performed by one holding proper authority. President Brigham Young taught: "It is supposed by this people that we have all the ordinances in our possession for life and salvation, and exaltation, and that we are administering these ordinances. This is not the case. We are in possession of all the ordinances that can be administered in the flesh [in mortality]; but there are other ordinances and administrations that must be administered beyond this world. I know you would ask what they are. I will mention one. We have not, neither can we receive here, the ordinance and the keys of the resurrection. They will be given to those who have passed off this stage of action and have received their bodies again, as many have already done and many more will. They will be ordained, by those who hold the keys of the resurrection, to go forth and resurrect the Saints, just as we receive the ordinance of baptism."[10] President Young also taught that "when the body comes forth again, it will be divine, God-like, according to the capacity and ordinations of the Lord."[11]

As to the process by which the resurrection will pass upon all, Elder Erastus Snow explained that "we have, in our limited understandings, perhaps imagined, many of us, that this glorious resurrection was to come upon us, and upon the whole world suddenly, like the rising of the sun. But you must remember the sun does not rise the same hour and the same moment upon all the earth. . . . So with the resurrection. There is a day appointed for the resurrection of the righteous. And it is sealed upon the heads of many that if they are faithful and true, they shall come forth 'in the morning of the first resurrection'; but the morning lasts from the first hour of the day until mid-day, and the day lasts till night; and the rest of the dead—those who are not prepared or counted worthy to have part in the first resurrection—shall not live again until the thousand years are ended." Elder Snow then added that those who come forth in the morning of the first resurrection "shall be crowned kings and priests with God and the Lamb—they shall reign with Christ . . . and carry on the work of redemption and resurrection of the Saints of God."[12]

AN ETERNAL PHYSICAL EXISTENCE

Unlike so many in the religious world, the Latter-day Saints anticipate celestial life on a material earth. Elder Orson Pratt eloquently made this point as follows: "A Saint who is one in deed and truth, does not look for an immaterial heaven, but he expects a heaven with lands, houses, cities, vegetation, rivers, and animals; with thrones, temples, palaces, kings, princes, priests, and angels; with food, raiment, musical instruments, etc., all of which are material. Indeed, the Saints' heaven is a redeemed, glorified, celestial, material creation, inhabited by glorified material beings, male and female, organized into families, embracing all the relationships of husbands and wives, parents and children, where sorrow, crying, pain, and death will be known no more. Or to speak still more definitely, this earth, when glorified, is the Saints' eternal heaven. On it they expect to live, with body, parts, and holy passions; on it they expect to move and have their being; to eat, drink, converse, worship, sing, play on musical instruments, engage in joyful, innocent, social amusements, visit neighboring

.towns and neighboring worlds; *indeed, matter and its qualities and properties are the only beings or things with which they expect to associate. . . .*

"Materiality is indelibly stamped upon the very heaven of heavens, upon all the eternal creations; it is the very essence of all existence."[13]

"All men know that they must die," the Prophet Joseph said at the funeral for James Adams. "And it is important that we should understand the reasons and causes of our exposure to the vicissitudes of life and of death, and the designs and purposes of God in our coming into the world, our sufferings here, and our departure hence. What is the object of our coming into existence, then dying and falling away, to be here no more? It is but reasonable to suppose that God would reveal something in reference to the matter, and it is a subject we ought to study more than any other. We ought to study it day and night, for the world is ignorant in reference to their true condition and relation. If we have any claim on our Heavenly Father for anything, it is for knowledge on this important subject."[14]

"More painful to me are the thoughts of annihilation than death," Joseph Smith once declared.[15] With the restoration of divine truths concerning life after death, light has replaced darkness, sound doctrine and pure religion have replaced ignorance and superstition, and individuals may now traverse life's paths without that ominous fear of what, if anything, follows death. We know where we came from. We know why we are here. And we know where we are going when death calls to each of us, when we pass through that veil that separates time and eternity. The testimony of holy writ resounds: in Christ there is peace. In Christ there is hope, hope for deliverance from sin and death. There are no wrongs that will not be righted in time or eternity, no burdens that will not be lifted. With a perspective informed by a panoramic vision, the Prophet of the Restoration promised: "All your losses will be made up to you in the resurrection, provided you continue faithful. By the vision of the Almighty I have seen it."[16] And thank God that Joseph saw it, for now we have a modern witness, linked with ancient scripture, that death is not the end but rather the beginning of eternal growth and everlasting progression.

Chapter 6

MANY MANSIONS
OF THE FATHER

$\mathcal{W}$hile meeting with his chosen disciples at the Last Supper, the Master said: "Let not your heart be troubled: ye believe in God, believe also in me. In my Father's house are many mansions: if it were not so, I would have told you. I go to prepare a place for you" (John 14:1–2). This is a most intriguing statement. The Savior seems to have been saying, in essence, that it should be obvious, self-evident, to anyone that life hereafter consists of more than merely a heaven and a hell; if it were not so, he would have told us otherwise. Reason suggests that not all people are equally good and thus not all good people deserve the same reward hereafter. Likewise, not all bad people are equally bad, and surely some are so bad they deserve to sink to the lowest pit in hell. Something so fundamental would surely be a part of what God would make known to his children.

THE VISION

In June 1830 the Prophet Joseph Smith began an inspired translation of the King James Version of the Bible, a labor to which he was divinely directed and appointed, a work he considered to be a "branch of [his] calling."[1] The Prophet and his scribes progressed through the book of Genesis until March 7, 1831, when the Lord commanded the Prophet to turn his attention to the New Testament (D&C 45:60–61). On September 12, 1831, to escape persecution, Joseph Smith relocated to Hiram, Ohio, to live with the John Johnson family.

By February 16, 1832, the Prophet and his scribe, Sidney Rigdon, had translated much of the fifth chapter of John. In verses 28 and 29 of that chapter, the Savior indicates that the time will come when the dead will hear the voice of the Son of God and will come forth from the graves: "They that have done good, unto the resurrection of life; and they that have done evil, unto the resurrection of damnation." The Prophet felt impressed to alter the text as follows: "And shall come forth; they who have done good, in the resurrection of *the just*; and they who have done evil, in the resurrection of *the unjust*" (JST, John 5:29; emphasis added; D&C 76:17). "Now this caused us to marvel," the Prophet stated, "for it was given unto us of the Spirit. And while we meditated upon these things, the Lord touched the eyes of our understandings and they were opened, and the glory of the Lord shone round about" (D&C 76:18–19). The alteration in the text, though interesting, is not earthshaking or overwhelming. But truly, "out of small things proceedeth that which is great" (D&C 64:33). There came to Joseph Smith and his scribe on that occasion one of the most remarkable visions ever recorded, one we have come to know simply as the vision, or the vision of the glories, which is recorded in Doctrine and Covenants 76. This grand revelation stands for Latter-day Saints as an interpretive commentary upon the Savior's words concerning "many mansions" in the world to come.

Philo Dibble, one who was in the Johnson home when the vision was received, has left us the following fascinating account:

"The vision of the three degrees of glory which is recorded in the Doctrine and Covenants was given at the house of 'Father Johnson,' in Hiram, Ohio, and during the time that Joseph and Sidney were in the Spirit and saw the heavens open there were other men in the room, perhaps twelve, among whom I was one during a part of the time—probably two-thirds of the time. I saw the glory and felt the power, but did not see the vision.

"Joseph wore black clothes, but at this time seemed to be dressed in an element of glorious white, and his face shone as if it were transparent, but I did not see the same glory attending Sidney. . . .

"Joseph would, at intervals, say: 'What do I see?' as one might say while looking out the window and beholding what all in the room could not see. Then he would relate what he had seen or what he was looking at.

"Then Sidney replied, 'I see the same.'

"Presently Sidney would say, 'What do I see?' and would repeat what he had seen or was seeing.

"And Joseph would reply, 'I see the same.'

"This manner of conversation was repeated at short intervals to the end of the vision, and during the whole time not a word was spoken by any other person. Not a sound or motion was made by anyone but Joseph and Sidney, and it seemed to me that they never moved a joint or limb during the time I was there, which I think was over an hour, and to the end of the vision.

"Joseph sat firmly and calmly all the time in the midst of a magnificent glory, but Sidney sat limp and pale, apparently as limber as a rag, observing which, Joseph remarked, smilingly, 'Sidney is not used to it as I am.'"[2]

After the vision closed and while still in the Spirit, the Prophet and his scribe were permitted to record a hundredth part of what they saw and experienced (compare D&C 76:115–16).[3] In fact, the vision actually consists of six visions, each of which we will now consider briefly.

THE GLORY OF THE SON

The first vision is the vision of the glory of the Son. It sets the stage for what follows by placing in perspective God's work of redemption and salvation—namely, that salvation is in Jesus Christ and comes through the shedding of his own blood and his glorious rise to newness of life in resurrection. The translators thus saw in vision "the glory of the Son, on the right hand of the Father, and received of his fulness; and saw the holy angels, and them who are sanctified before his throne, worshiping God, and the Lamb, who worship him forever and ever" (D&C 76:20–21). John the Revelator had similarly recorded concerning the Redeemer, "And the number of [angels] was ten thousand times ten thousand, and thousands of thousands; saying with a loud voice, Worthy is the Lamb that was slain to receive power, and riches, and wisdom, and strength, and honour, and glory, and blessing" (Revelation 5:11–12).

The Prophet and his scribe bore witness of the Redeemer in powerful language: "And now, after the many testimonies which have been given of him, this is the testimony, last of all, which we give of him: That he lives! For we saw him, even on the right hand of God; and we heard the voice bearing record that he is the Only Begotten of the Father—That by him, and through him, and of him, the worlds are and were created, and the inhabitants thereof are begotten sons and daughters unto God" (D&C 76:22–24). Truly, the "testimony of Jesus is the spirit of prophecy" (Revelation 19:10), and all the holy prophets, from the beginning, have testified of the One who called and sent them (Acts 10:43; Jacob 4:4; 7:11; Mosiah 13:33).

In addition, the Prophet Joseph's witness contains significant doctrine. For one thing, his testimony affirms the burden of scripture, that Jehovah—Christ—was and is the Creator of worlds without number (Moses 1:33; 7:30; Ephesians 3:9; Hebrews 1:1–2). It confirms also the infinite and eternal nature of the Atonement. Whatsoever our Lord and Master creates, he redeems. That is to say, his redemptive labors reach beyond the bounds of our earth (Moses 1:32–35).

In a poetic version of the vision written in 1843, verses 22 through 24 were rendered as follows:

> And now after all of the proofs made of him,
> By witnesses truly, but whom he was known,
> This is mine, last of all, that he lives; yea he lives!
> And sits at the right hand of God, on his throne.
> And I heard a great voice, bearing record from heav'n,
> He's the Savior, and only begotten of God—
> By him, of him, and through him, the worlds were all made,
> Even all that career in the heavens so broad,
> Whose inhabitants, too, from the first to the last,
> Are sav'd by the very same Saviour of ours;
> And, of course, are begotten God's daughters and sons,
> By the very same truths, and the very same pow'rs.[4]

As Elder Russell M. Nelson pointed out, Christ's Atonement "is infinite—without an end. It was also infinite in that all humankind would be saved from never-ending death. It was infinite in terms of His immense suffering. It was infinite in time, putting an end to the preceding prototype of animal sacrifice. It was infinite in scope—it was to be done once for all. And the mercy of the Atonement extends not only to an infinite number of people, but also to an infinite number of worlds created by Him."[5]

THE FALL OF LUCIFER

The second vision is a vision of the fall of Lucifer. Having been shown that the foundation of our faith is redemption in Christ, the Prophet and Sidney Rigdon learned a vital element of the plan of salvation—the nature of opposition through Satan and satanic influences. Lucifer is described in the vision as one "who was in authority in the presence of God" (D&C 76:25), who rebelled against the Father and the Son in the premortal council in heaven, thus becoming known as *perdition*, meaning "ruin" or "destruction." He is our spirit brother, "a son of the morning," one over whom "the heavens wept" (D&C 76:26). He coveted the throne of the Father and proposed to save all the sons and daughters of God in a way contrary to the plan of the Father (Moses 4:1–4). "The contention in heaven was—Jesus said there would be certain souls that would not be saved; and the devil said he would save them all, and laid his plans before the grand council, who gave their vote in favor of Jesus Christ. So the devil rose up in rebellion against God, and was cast down, with all who put up their heads for him."[6] Lucifer became thereby an enemy to God and to all righteousness: "Wherefore, he maketh war with the saints of God, and encompasseth them round about" (D&C 76:25–29).

THE SONS OF PERDITION

The third vision is a vision of the sons of perdition. Doctrine and Covenants 76:30–49 describes those who have once known light and truth and the revelations of heaven and who nevertheless choose knowingly to deny the light and defy God and his work. These are the sons of perdition, "vessels of wrath, doomed to suffer the wrath of God, with the devil and his angels in eternity" (D&C 76:33). The apostle Paul observed that "it is impossible for those who were once enlightened, and have tasted of the heavenly gift, and were made partakers of the Holy Ghost, and have tasted the good word of God, and the powers of the world to come, if they shall fall away, to renew them again unto repentance" (Hebrews 6:4–6; compare 10:26–29).

"What must a man do to commit the unpardonable sin?" Joseph the Seer asked in the King Follett sermon. "He must receive the Holy Ghost, have the heavens opened unto him, and know God, and then sin against Him. After a man has sinned against the Holy Ghost, there is no repentance for him. He has got to say that the sun does not shine while he sees it; he has got to deny Jesus Christ when the heavens have been opened unto him, and to deny the plan of salvation with his eyes open to the truth of it; and from that time he begins to be an enemy." He continued: "When a man begins to be an enemy to this work, he hunts me, he seeks to kill me, and never ceases to thirst for my blood. He gets the spirit of the devil—the same spirit that they had who crucified the Lord of Life—the same spirit that sins against the Holy Ghost. You cannot save such persons; you cannot bring them to repentance; they make open war, like the devil, and awful is the consequence."[7]

All the sons and daughters of Adam and Eve will come forth from the grave in the resurrection, including sons of perdition (D&C 88:32). The sons of perdition are guilty of the unpardonable sin (Alma 39:6), a sin not covered by the Atonement of Christ, a sin for which no amount of personal suffering can right the wrong. There is no forgiveness for those who commit that unpardonable sin, neither here nor hereafter, for "having denied the Holy Spirit after having received it, and having denied the

Only Begotten Son of the Father, having crucified him unto themselves and put him to an open shame" (D&C 76:34–35), they are guilty of shedding innocent blood, meaning the innocent blood of Christ. "The blasphemy against the Holy Ghost," a later revelation affirms, "which shall not be forgiven in the world nor out of the world, is in that ye commit murder wherein ye shed innocent blood, and *assent unto my death*, after ye have received my new and everlasting covenant, saith the Lord God" (D&C 132:27; emphasis added). The sons of perdition are the only ones who will be subject to the second spiritual death, the final expulsion from the presence of God. They, after being resurrected and standing before God to be judged (2 Nephi 9:15), will be consigned to a kingdom of no glory.

In the midst of this gloomy scene, the Lord provides a most beautiful description of the gospel of Jesus Christ, the "glad tidings" that "he came into the world, even Jesus, to be crucified for the world, and to bear the sins of the world, and to sanctify the world, and to cleanse it from all unrighteousness; that through him all might be saved whom the Father had put into his power and made by him; who glorifies the Father, and saves all the works of his hands, except those sons of perdition who deny the Son after the Father has revealed him" (D&C 76:40–43).

This third vision ends with a sobering reminder that the particulars of the fate of the sons of perdition have not been revealed (D&C 76:45–48). In 1833 the Prophet Joseph Smith explained that "the Lord never authorized [certain individuals] to say that the devil, his angels or the sons of perdition, should ever be restored; for their state of destiny was not revealed to man, is not revealed, nor ever shall be revealed, save to those who are made partakers thereof: consequently those who teach this doctrine, have not received it of the Spirit of the Lord. Truly Brother Oliver declared it to be the doctrine of devils."[8]

THE CELESTIAL GLORY

The fourth vision is the vision of the celestial glory. As this vision unfolded, the Prophet and Sidney were permitted to study and learn by contrast—from perdition to exaltation. They beheld the glories of the highest, or celestial, kingdom and provided broad descriptions of those who inhabit it. They saw the participants in the "resurrection of the just" (D&C 76:50), which is what we call the first resurrection (Mosiah 15:21–25), the resurrection of celestial and terrestrial persons. Celestial persons are those who receive the testimony of Jesus and accept the terms and conditions of the gospel covenant. They are "baptized after the manner of his burial" and receive the gift of the Holy Ghost, thereby becoming "cleansed from all their sins" (D&C 76:51–52).

Those who inherit a celestial glory are they who "overcome by faith" (D&C 76:53), who "withstand every temptation of the devil, with their faith on the Lord Jesus Christ" (Alma 37:33). They overcome the world in forsaking worldliness and carnal attractions and give themselves to the Lord and his work. They are "sealed by the Holy Spirit of promise, which the Father sheds forth upon all those who are just and true" (D&C 76:53). The Holy Spirit of Promise is the Holy Ghost, the Holy Spirit promised to the Saints. Because "the Comforter knoweth all things" (D&C 42:17; Moses 6:61), the Holy Ghost is able to search the souls of individuals to ascertain the degree to which they have truly yielded their hearts unto God, the degree to which they are "just and true" (D&C 76:53). Thus, to be sealed by the Holy Spirit of Promise is to have the ratifying approval of the Holy

Ghost upon our lives and upon the ordinances and covenants into which we have entered. It is to have passed the tests of mortality, to have qualified for celestial glory hereafter:

> For these overcome, by their faith and their works,
> Being tried in their life-time, as purified gold,
> And seal'd by the spirit of promise, to life,
> By men called of God, as Aaron of old.[9]

Celestial men and women are "the church of the Firstborn" (D&C 76:54). The Church of the Firstborn is the "inner circle" of faithful Saints who have proven true and faithful to their covenants. Just as baptism is the gate to membership in the Church of Jesus Christ on earth, so celestial marriage opens the door to membership in the heavenly church.[10] The Church of the Firstborn is the Church beyond the veil, the organized body of Saints who inherit exaltation. It is made up of those who qualify for the blessings of the Firstborn. Jesus is the Firstborn of the Father and as such is entitled to the birthright. As an act of consummate mercy and grace, our loving Savior makes it possible for us to inherit, receive, and possess the same blessings he receives, as though each of us were the Firstborn. Those who come into the Church and live worthy of the companionship of the Holy Ghost are born again; they become the sons and daughters of Jesus Christ by adoption (Mosiah 5:1–7). If they continue faithful, receive thereafter the covenants and ordinances of the temple (including the endowment and celestial marriage), and are true to those higher covenants, they will eventually become the sons and daughters of God, meaning the Father.[11] They become heirs of God and joint heirs, or coinheritors, with Christ to all that the Father has, including eternal life. "Wherefore, as it is written, they are gods, even the sons of God" (D&C 76:58). President

Brigham Young stated, therefore, that "the ordinances of the house of God are expressly for the Church of the Firstborn."[12]

"They are they who are priests and kings, who have received of his fulness, and of his glory" (D&C 76:56). That is, they are kings and queens, priests and priestesses, men and women who through their steadfastness and immovability in keeping their covenants have received what the prophets call the "fulness of the priesthood" (D&C 124:28). The Prophet Joseph explained in 1843 that "those holding the fullness of the Melchizedek Priesthood are kings and priests of the Most High God, holding the keys of power and blessings."[13] These are they who will accompany the Master when he returns in glory, those who, if they have already passed through the veil of death, will come forth from the grave in glorious immortality. The first resurrection, which began at the time of Christ's resurrection, will thus resume. These are they whose names are written in heaven, in the Lamb's book of life (D&C 88:2), "where God and Christ are the judge of all" (D&C 76:68).

And then, lest we should conclude that such persons have attained to this highest degree of glory on their own through their own merits and mortal accomplishments, or without divine assistance, the holy word attests: "These are they who are *just men made perfect through Jesus the mediator of the new covenant, who* wrought out this perfect atonement through the shedding of his own blood" (D&C 76:69; emphasis added). They are *made perfect*—whole, complete, fully formed, spiritually mature—through their covenant union with the Savior.

THE TERRESTRIAL GLORY

The fifth vision, a vision of the terrestrial glory, represents a continuation of the first resurrection, or the resurrection of the just. The Prophet and his scribe witnessed the final state of those who chose to abide by goodness and equity and decency in their second estate but chose also not to receive and incorporate the fulness of that light and power that derive from receiving the everlasting gospel. The terrestrial world is inhabited by those who in this life did not receive the testimony of Jesus—the testimony that he is the Savior and Redeemer of mankind—but afterward received it; that is, they received that witness in the postmortal spirit world (D&C 76:73–74). The terrestrial world is also inhabited by those who knew in this life that Jesus was the Christ but who were not valiant enough in that witness to receive the fulness of the gospel when it was presented to them. Or, as it is rendered poetically:

> Not valiant for truth, they obtain'd not the crown,
> But are of that glory that's typ'd by the moon:
> They are they, that come into the presence of Christ,
> But not to the fulness of God, on his throne.[14]

For that matter, those who have received the fulness of the gospel of Jesus Christ—in our day, those who have joined The Church of Jesus Christ of Latter-day Saints—and then do not prove to be valiant in their testimony are candidates for the terrestrial degree of glory hereafter.

THE TELESTIAL GLORY

Remembering that celestial persons receive both the testimony of Jesus and the gospel covenant and that terrestrial persons receive the testimony of Jesus but not the gospel covenant, we learn in vision six concerning the inhabitants of the telestial world: "These are they who received not the gospel of Christ, neither the testimony of Jesus" (D&C 76:82; see also D&C 76:101). They "deny not the Holy Spirit" (D&C 76:83). That is, their wickedness is not such as to lead to complete perdition; they are not guilty of the unpardonable sin, but they are "thrust down to hell" (D&C 76:84); at the time of their mortal death, they enter into that realm of the postmortal sphere we know as hell and are confronted with their sinfulness. These do not come forth from the grave until the "last resurrection," until the end of the Millennium, "until the Lord, even Christ the Lamb, shall have finished his work" (D&C 76:85).

As is the case with the other kingdoms of glory, there are broad classifications of telestial people. "These are they who are of Paul, and of Apollos, and of Cephas. These are they who say they are some of one and some of another—some of Christ and some of John, and some of Moses, and some of Elias, and some of Esaias, and some of Isaiah, and some of Enoch; but received not the gospel, neither the testimony of Jesus, neither the prophets, neither the everlasting covenant" (D&C 76:99–101). Or, as it is stated poetically,

> These are they that came out for Apollos and Paul;
> For Cephas and Jesus, in all kinds of hope;
> For Enoch and Moses, and Peter, and John;
> For Luther and Calvin, and even the Pope.
> For they never received the gospel of Christ,
> Nor the prophetic spirit that came from the Lord;
> Nor the covenant neither, which Jacob once had;
> They went their own way, and they have their reward.[15]

Further, the telestial kingdom is the final abode of liars, sorcerers, adulterers, and whoremongers, and, as John the Revelator learned, of murderers (D&C 76:103; Revelation 21:8; 22:15).

Finally, the vision adds the sobering detail that the inhabitants of the telestial world, "as innumerable as the stars in the firmament of heaven, or as the sand upon the seashore," will be "servants of the Most High; but where God and Christ dwell they cannot come, worlds without end" (D&C 76:109, 112).

In short, the celestial body is qualitatively different from the terrestrial or the telestial body. Elder Melvin J. Ballard pointed out that "one who gains possession of the lowest degree of the telestial glory may ultimately rise to the highest degree of that glory, but no provision has been made for promotion from one glory to another. . . . Those who come forth in the celestial glory with celestial bodies have a body that is more refined. It is different. . . . When we have a celestial body it will be suited to the celestial conditions, and telestial bodies could not endure celestial glory. It would be torment and affliction to them. I have not read in the scripture where there will be another resurrection where we can obtain a celestial body for a terrestrial body. What we receive in the resurrection will be ours forever and forever."[16]

"The celestial and terrestrial and telestial glories, I have heard compared to the wheels on a train," said President Joseph Fielding Smith. "The second and third may, and will, reach the place where the first was, but the first will have moved on and will still be just the same distance in advance of them. *This illustration is not true! The wheels do not run on the same track, and do not go in the same direction. The terrestrial and the telestial are limited in their powers of advancement, worlds without end.*"[17]

Likewise, President Spencer W. Kimball taught: "After a person has been assigned to his place in the kingdom, either in the telestial, the terrestrial or the celestial, or to his exaltation, he will never advance from his assigned glory to another glory. That is eternal! That is why we must make our decisions early in life and why it is imperative that such decisions be right."[18]

Although the telestial kingdom is the lowest of the kingdoms of glory, the inhabitants of that glory will be "heirs of salvation" in a world that "surpasses all understanding" (D&C 76:88–89). Generally speaking, the word *salvation* means in scripture exactly the same thing as *exaltation* or *eternal life* (D&C 6:13; 14:7; Alma 11:40). There are a couple of times in scripture, however, when *salvation* refers to something less than exaltation (see, for example, D&C 132:17), and the vision of the glories is one of those times. Our Lord seeks to save all of his children with an everlasting salvation. And he does so in that all but the sons of perdition eventually inherit a kingdom of glory (D&C 76:43). In fact, President Charles W. Penrose observed about the telestial kingdom: "While there is one soul of this race, willing and able to accept and obey the laws of redemption, no matter where or in what condition it may be found, *Christ's work will be incomplete until that being is brought* up from death and hell, and placed in a position of progress, upward and onward, in such glory as is possible for its enjoyment and the service of the great God.

"The punishment inflicted will be adequate to the wrongs performed. In one sense the sinner will always suffer its effects. When the debt is paid and justice is satisfied; when obedience is learned through the lessons of sad experience; when the grateful and subdued soul comes forth from the everlasting punishment, thoroughly willing to comply with the laws once rejected; there will be an abiding sense of loss. The fulness of celestial glory in the presence and society of God and the Lamb are beyond the reach of that saved but not perfected soul, forever. The power of increase, wherein are dominion and exaltation and crowns of immeasurable glory, is not for the class of beings who have been thrust down to hell and endured the wrath of God for the period allotted by eternal judgment. . . .

"Those who were cast down to the depths for their sins, who

rejected the gospel of Jesus, who persecuted the saints, who reveled in iniquity, who committed all manner of transgressions except the unpardonable crime, will also come forth in the Lord's time, through the blood of the Lamb and the ministry of His disciples and their own repentance and willing acceptance of divine law, and enter into the various degrees of glory and power and progress and light, according to their different capacities and adaptabilities. They cannot go up into the society of the Father nor receive of the presence of the Son, but will have ministrations of messengers from the terrestrial world, and *have joy beyond all expectations and the conception of uninspired mortal minds*. They will all bow the knee to Christ and serve God the Father, and have an eternity of usefulness and happiness in harmony with the higher powers. They receive the telestial glory."[19]

THE RESTORATION CONTINUES

The Prophet Joseph Smith and Sidney Rigdon received the vision of the glories in 1832. God continued to reveal himself, his plan, and the doctrines of salvation during the next twelve years of the Prophet's mortal ministry and subsequently to his successors. Some time after the coming of Elijah and the restoration of the sealing power and the fulness of the priesthood in April 1836, the Prophet Joseph Smith introduced the Saints to the doctrine and practice of celestial marriage. He taught that "in the celestial glory there are three heavens or degrees; and in order to obtain the highest, a man must enter into this order of the priesthood [meaning the new and everlasting covenant of marriage]; and if he does not, he cannot obtain it. He may enter into the other, but that is the end of his kingdom; he cannot have an increase" (D&C 131:1–4). Or, as the Prophet stated another way, "Except a man and his wife enter into an everlasting covenant and be married for eternity, while in this probation, by the power and authority of the Holy Priesthood, they will cease to increase when they die; that is, they will not have any children after the resurrection. But those who are married by the power and authority of the priesthood in this life, and continue without committing the sin against the Holy Ghost, will continue to increase and have children in the celestial glory."[20]

So just how strange, how unusual, is this belief in varying degrees of reward hereafter? Popular Evangelical Christian writer Bruce Wilkinson wrote: "Although your eternal destination is based on your belief [in Jesus Christ as Lord and Savior], how you spend eternity is based on your behavior while on earth." Thus Dr. Wilkinson's "Unbreakable Link" is described as follows: "Your choices on earth have direct consequences on your life in eternity." Because discipleship flows from true conversion, "doing is a servant's language of devotion."[21] In short, "there will be varying degrees of reward in heaven."[22]

St. Augustine, perhaps the most significant influence on both Roman Catholic and Protestant theology, wrote: "But who can conceive, not to say describe, what degrees of honor and glory shall be awarded to the various degrees of merit? Yet *it cannot be doubted that there shall be degrees.* And in that blessed city there shall be this great blessing, that no inferior shall envy any superior, as now the archangels are not envied by the angels, because *no one will wish to be what he has not received,* though bound in strictest concord with him who has received; as in the body the finger does not seek to be the eye, though both members are harmoniously included in the complete structure of the body. And thus, along with this gift, greater or less, each shall receive this further gift of contentment to desire no more than he has."[23]

During the First Great Awakening, American theologian

Jonathan Edwards stated that "there are many mansions in God's house because heaven is intended for various degrees of honor and blessedness. Some are designed to sit in higher places there than others; some are designed to be advanced to higher degrees of honor and glory than others are."[24] Similarly, John Wesley, the father of Methodism, spoke of some persons enjoying "higher degrees of glory" hereafter. "There is an inconceivable variety in the degrees of reward in the other world. . . . In worldly things, men are ambitious to get as high as they can. Christians have a far more noble ambition. The difference between the very highest and the lowest state in the world is nothing to the smallest difference between the degrees of glory."[25]

A SOLID AND SOUL-SATISFYING DOCTRINE

Not long ago I found myself sitting on an airplane beside a man with whom I struck up a conversation. The man, whose name was Dave, explained that he was a member of the Church, had been baptized nine years ago, and was overwhelmed with gratitude for the restored gospel in his life. I asked how he had come into the Church. He replied that he had been brought up in a home where both of his parents were conservative Protestants, Evangelical Christians. Ten years ago he found himself wondering about his own spiritual state, whether he would go to heaven when he died. In fact, he said, he began to be almost obsessed with the idea of heaven and found himself reading and thinking about it constantly. He even noticed that within a very short period of time he heard a particular contemporary Christian song that spoke a great deal about heaven played on the radio several times. One day he found himself in company with a friend who, he discovered, had become acquainted with the Mormon missionaries in the area. The friend had played basketball with them on their preparation day. The friend commented about some of the unusual beliefs of the Latter-day Saints, and Dave asked his friend to be more specific. The friend observed that Mormons believed there were more heavens than one, that there were degrees of glory. Dave responded, "That's exactly what I believe!" After prayerfully studying and contemplating on the matter, Dave had come to the conclusion that this had to be the case, that people were different, that there must be varying rewards in heaven hereafter. Dave then spoke with the missionaries himself, accepted their message, and was baptized.

The vision is a remarkable oracle, an unparalleled manifestation of the mercy and love of our Eternal Father and his Beloved Son. "Nothing could be more pleasing to the Saints upon the order of the kingdom of the Lord," Joseph Smith stated, "than the light which burst upon the world through the foregoing vision. Every law, every commandment, every promise, every truth, and every point touching the destiny of man, from Genesis to Revelation, . . . witnesses the fact that the document is a transcript from the records of the eternal world. The sublimity of the ideas; the purity of the language; the scope for action; the continued duration for completion, in order that the heirs of salvation may confess the Lord and bow the knee; the rewards for faithfulness, and the punishments for sins, are so much beyond the narrow-mindedness of men, that every honest man is constrained to exclaim: '*It came from God.*'"[26]

Truly there are many mansions of the Father (John 14:2), and the Holy One of Israel has made provision for his people to attain to that level of glory hereafter that they are willing to receive. The Prophet quoted the Savior about many mansions and said: "It should be—'In my Father's kingdom are many kingdoms,' in order that ye may be heirs of God and joint-heirs with me. I do not believe the Methodist doctrine of sending honest men and noble-minded men to hell, along with the murderer and the adulterer. They may hurl all their hell and fiery billows upon me, for they will roll off me as fast as they come on. But I have an order of things to save the poor fellows at any rate, and get them saved; for I will send men to preach to them in prison and save them if I can."[27] Here is a message of hope, a breath of fresh air amid the fiery winds of sectarian theology, a doctrine that manifests transformatively the grace and wisdom of our Divine Redeemer.

Chapter 7

SALVATION, EXALTATION, AND ETERNAL LIFE

$\mathcal{S}$o often we read through the scriptures—day in and day out, week after week and month after month, from start to finish—and seldom take the time to step back, ponder and reflect on the larger themes and doctrinal refrains that work their way through the scriptures and the history of the Church.

A DISTILLATION EXPRESSION

Through the years I have found it especially helpful in teaching the Book of Mormon to returned missionaries, for example, to walk into class the first day and distribute copies of questions that will appear on the final examination. The students are generally stunned. They wonder why we would be contemplating the end while we are just at the beginning. Some of the questions I distribute include the following:

- "Explain how the Book of Mormon is a 'history of a fallen people.'"
- "Discuss how the Book of Mormon does indeed teach 'what great things the Lord hath done' for our fathers."
- "Given more than a thousand years of history and experience within the pages of the Book of Mormon, what

counsel would you offer to the rising generation on how to avoid the perils of the prosperity cycle?"

• "Discuss the prophetic/editorial role of Mormon and how he helped to achieve the overarching purposes of the Book of Mormon."

• "How do the Book of Mormon prophets establish in the minds of people in their day—as well as in our own time— that 'Jesus is the Christ, the Eternal God'?"

Such questions cause us to think deeply and broadly, comprehensively, to move beyond the specifics and assess the larger, more far-reaching messages. They move us toward viewing God and his gospel from a more elevated and grand perspective. Likewise, we might distil the message of a specific book of scripture such as Leviticus by turning to a single verse: "The life of the flesh is in the blood. . . . It is the blood that maketh an atonement for the soul" (Leviticus 17:11). With all the numerous and varied details that we encounter in Leviticus, including the many sacrificial offerings described in that rather challenging text, that effort to find the overall message in a single verse enables us to gain a better view of things. We may not be able to define or distinguish among burnt offerings, meal offerings, peace offerings, sin offerings, or trespass offerings, but we can begin to sense what is behind it all, what God would have us see and understand about the sufferings and death and atoning mercies of his Son, the Holy Messiah.

Could we find a grander and more comprehensive expression, a more powerful distillation of what the Lord God is all about than the one he delivered to Moses the Lawgiver on the unnamed mountain? After having allowed Moses to see the earth— every particle and every person on it—and after speaking of the fact that worlds without end have "passed away by the word of

[his] power," Moses heard these timeless and theologically pro-found words: "For behold, this is my work and my glory—to bring to pass the immortality and eternal life of man" (Moses 1:35, 39).

There it is—the summation of it all, the *why* behind the how of God's creative and redemptive enterprise. God and Christ are in the business of people. The great plan of happiness is indeed the plan of salvation, the heaven-ordained program by which such weak and fallen creatures as ourselves can be forgiven, cleansed, renewed, reinstated, restored, and returned to the divine presence, all through the love and condescension and mediation of the Holy Messiah. There is nothing that is of greater worth to our Heavenly Father and his Beloved Son than are you and I, his children.

SCRIPTURAL DEFINITIONS

To possess the gift of *immortality* is to have the power to live forever, the capacity to endure every obstacle to life. The scriptures speak expressly of immortality as one of the wondrous gifts to man through the atonement of Jesus Christ. And yet, as Latter-day Saints we recognize that the spirit of man is already an immortal entity, a conscious personality that never began and cannot cease to exist. Even if there had been no Atonement, the spirit of man would live on everlastingly. But the immortality of which the scriptures speak is that immortality associated with the immortal soul, or the resurrected body—the inseparable union of body and spirit equipped thereafter for a kingdom of glory. Only through the actions of a God—the redemptive labors of Jesus the Christ—can such an immortal state be attained. "Now if we be dead with Christ," Paul taught, "we believe that we shall also live with him: Knowing that Christ being raised from the dead dieth no more; death hath no more dominion over him. For in that he died, he died unto sin once: but in that he liveth, he liveth unto God" (Romans 6:8–10).

Amulek's description of the resurrected body uses the word *spiritual* synonymously with the word *immortal* (Alma 11:45). This usage appears to be common to prophets of all the ages to denote a state that is not subject to death (compare 1 Corinthians 15:44; D&C 88:27; Moses 3:9). Immortality is a free gift to all who qualify for the second estate, a supernal grace that requires neither righteousness nor rigorous attention to God's laws: "For as in Adam all die, even so in Christ shall all be made alive" (1 Corinthians 15:22). We cannot improve upon Amulek's expression: "Now, *this restoration* [of body and spirit] *shall come to all*, both old and young, both bond and free, both male and female, both the wicked and the righteous" (Alma 11:44; emphasis added).

Eternal life is the kind of life enjoyed by our Father in Heaven; it is God's life (see Moses 7:35). It consists primarily of two conditions: (1) inheriting, receiving, and possessing the fulness of the glory of the Father; and (2) a continuation of the family unit in eternity (D&C 132:19). Immortality is a free gift to all, but eternal life is something that comes only through faith in the Lord Jesus Christ, including the actions that proceed from faith—repentance, baptism, and diligent discipleship. Both of these conditions are made available through our Lord's suffering in Gethsemane and on Golgotha, as well as his rise to glorious immortality from the garden tomb.

In a way incomprehensible to mortal and finite minds, our Savior's conquest of physical death—his rise from the tomb into resurrected glory—is passed along to all mortals: Because he rose, so we all will likewise rise, each in his or her appointed time and order. Immortality, the measure of the *quantity* of an everlasting life, is thus a reality.

Also inexplicable is the manner in which our Deliverer descended below all things and took upon him the weight and effects of the sins of all humankind, making repentance and forgiveness available to the penitent. Eternal life, an expression descriptive of the *quality* of one's immortality, is thus also a reality and a possibility for those who accept and apply the principles of the gospel of Jesus Christ.

Having spoken in a modern revelation of the creation and fall of Adam, the Lord observed: "And thus did I, the Lord God, appoint unto man the days of his probation—*that by his natural death he might be raised in immortality unto eternal life*, even as many as would believe" (D&C 29:43; emphasis added). Paul wrote to Timothy of our Master as he "who hath abolished death, and hath brought [eternal] life and immortality to light through the gospel" (2 Timothy 1:10).

"Salvation consists in the glory, authority, majesty, power and dominion which Jehovah possesses and in nothing else; and no being can possess it but himself or one like him."[1] So taught Joseph Smith to the School of the Prophets in the winter of 1834–35. Both the Prophet of the Restoration and Paul the Apostle taught that Jesus Christ had gained salvation because he had put all enemies under his feet, the last enemy being death. It is just so with all men and women: We will gain salvation as we, through the power of Christ's atonement, are enabled to place all enemies, including death, beneath our feet.[2]

Salvation is eternal life. It is life in the highest heaven, life among the Gods and the angels. The word *salvation* means exactly the same thing as *eternal life* but simply emphasizes one's saved condition, one's healing and deliverance, deliverance from death and sin through the atoning sacrifice of Jesus Christ. *Exaltation* is another word with which we have come to identify the glories of the celestial kingdom; *exaltation* has the same meaning as *eternal life* and the same meaning as *salvation*. To be saved is to be exalted, the term *exaltation* simply laying stress upon the elevated and ennobled status of one who qualifies to dwell with and be a part of an eternal family forever and to inherit membership in the Church of the Firstborn, the Church of the exalted. Elder Bruce R. McConkie wrote: "We are ofttimes prone to create artificial distinctions, to say that salvation means one thing and exaltation another, to suppose that salvation means to be resurrected, but that exaltation or eternal life is something in addition thereto. It is true that there are some passages of scripture that use salvation in a special and limited sense in order to give an overall perspective of the plan of salvation that we would not otherwise have (2 Nephi 9:1–27; D&C 76:40–49; 132:15–17). These passages show the difference between general or universal salvation that consists in coming forth from the grave in immortality, and specific or individual salvation that consists of an inheritance in the celestial kingdom. . . .

"Since it is the prophetic purpose to lead men to full salvation in the highest heaven of the celestial world, when they speak and write about salvation, almost without exception, they mean eternal life or exaltation. They use the terms salvation, exaltation, and eternal life as synonyms, as words that mean exactly the same thing without any difference, distinction, or variance whatever."[3]

Amulek certainly equated the two terms *eternal life* and *salvation*. He said concerning the coming of the Messiah: "And he shall come into the world to redeem his people; and he shall take upon him the transgressions of those who believe on his name; and *these are they that shall have eternal life, and salvation cometh to none else*" (Alma 11:40; emphasis added). In a revelation given to the Prophet Joseph Smith and Oliver Cowdery, the Savior said, "If thou wilt do good, yea, and hold out faithful to the end, thou shalt be saved in the kingdom of God, which is the greatest of all the gifts of God; for *there is no gift greater than the gift of salvation*" (D&C 6:13; emphasis added). Two months later the Lord spoke to David Whitmer: "And, if you keep my commandments and endure to the end *you shall have eternal life, which gift is the greatest of all the gifts of God*" (D&C 14:7; emphasis added).

The scriptures thus speak of one qualifying for the blessing of *eternal lives* (see D&C 132:22–25). To have eternal lives is to possess eternal life in the highest degree of the celestial kingdom, to be worthy of salvation, and to be a candidate for exaltation. The phrase *eternal lives* simply emphasizes the right of a worthy man and woman to enjoy "a continuation of the seeds," the everlasting perpetuation of the family unit (D&C 132:19).

There is no ceiling on the number of saved beings in eternity. The design of God's plan is to save all who will be saved. We state as an article of our faith: "We believe that through the Atonement of Christ, *all mankind may be saved*, by obedience to the laws and ordinances of the Gospel" (Articles of Faith 1:3; emphasis added). No person was promised eternal life in premortality on an unconditional basis, and likewise no soul was condemned as reprobate even before the foundations of the earth were laid.[4] In the words of Lehi to his son Jacob, "salvation is free" (2 Nephi 2:4), meaning that it is freely available to all. In addition, it is not something we can purchase by our good works; an infinite price has already been paid, even the precious blood of Christ (1 Corinthians 6:19–20; 7:23; 1 Peter 1:18–19). Our God does not operate by some secret agenda, for his plan and his purposes are available and accessible to all. Nephi taught that "the Lord God worketh not in darkness." Further, "he doeth not anything save it be for the benefit of the world; for he loveth the world, even that he layeth down his own life that he may draw all men unto him. Wherefore, he commandeth none that they shall not partake of his salvation." Emphatically, Nephi declared: "Hath he commanded any that they should not partake of his salvation? Behold I say unto you, Nay; but he hath given it free for all men; and he hath commanded his people that they should persuade all men to repentance" (2 Nephi 26:23–24, 27).

A REASON FOR HOPE AND OPTIMISM

The scriptures speak often of a "strait gate" and a "narrow way," which lead unto that life we have come to know as eternal life. Emphasis is frequently placed upon the fact that "few" will ultimately get onto the path and navigate the course that leads to a saved condition hereafter. "Strait is the gate, and narrow the way that leadeth unto the exaltation and continuation of the lives, and few there be that find it, because ye receive me not in the world neither do ye know me." On the other hand, "broad is the gate, and wide the way that leadeth to the deaths; and many there are that go in thereat, because they receive me not, neither do they abide in my law" (D&C 132:22, 25; compare Matthew 7:13).

These are scriptural passages that must be viewed in the proper perspective. In the long run, we must ever keep in mind that our God and Father is a successful parent and that he will save far more of his children than we suppose. If those words seem startling at first, let us reason for a moment. In comparison to the number of wicked souls at any given time, perhaps the number of faithful followers seems small. But we must keep in mind how many of our spirit brothers and sisters—an almost infinite number—will be saved. What of the children who died before the age of accountability—perhaps billions of little ones from the days of Adam to the time of the Millennium? What of the billions of those who never had opportunity to hear the gospel message in mortality but who afterwards received the glad tidings because of a disposition that hungered and thirsted after righteousness?

And, might we ask, What of the vast numbers of the children of God who qualified for exaltation from Enoch's city, from Melchizedek's Salem, or from the golden era of the Nephites? What of the countless billions of those children to be born during the great millennial era—during a time, as we have seen, when disease and death have no sting nor victory over mankind? That is the season when "children shall grow up without sin unto salvation" (D&C 45:58). Given the renewed and paradisiacal state of the earth, it may be that more persons who are of at least a terrestrial nature will live on the earth during the thousand years of our Lord's reign than the total of all who have lived during the previous six thousand years of the earth's temporal continuance. Indeed, who can count the number of saved beings in eternity? Our God, who is triumphant in all battles against the forces of evil, will surely be triumphant in the number of his children who will be saved.

It is vital that we as Latter-day Saints have hope, that we point and align and rivet ourselves on that goal of eternal life, despite our imperfections. Gaining salvation and attaining perfection are processes, lengthy processes that will go on even beyond death (D&C 93:19).

There are no instant Christians, no sudden disciples. In speaking to the youth of the Church, Elder Bruce R. McConkie taught the following vital and invigorating lessons: "We do not work out our salvation in a moment; it doesn't come to us in an instant, suddenly. Gaining salvation is a process. Paul says, 'Work out your own salvation with fear and trembling' (Philippians 2:12). To some members of the Church who had been baptized and who were on the course leading to eternal life, he said, 'Now is our salvation nearer than when we believed' (Romans 13:11). That is, 'We have made some progress along the straight and narrow path. We are going forward, and if we continue in that direction, eternal life will be our everlasting reward. . . . '

"As members of the Church, if we chart a course leading to eternal life; if we begin the processes of spiritual rebirth, and are going in the right direction; if we chart a course of sanctifying our souls, and degree by degree are going in that direction; and if we chart a course of becoming perfect, and, step by step and phase by phase, are perfecting our souls by overcoming the world, then it is absolutely guaranteed—there is no question whatever about it—we shall gain eternal life. Even though we have spiritual rebirth ahead of us, perfection ahead of us, the full degree of sanctification ahead of us, if we chart a course and follow it to the best of our ability in this life, then when we go out of this life we'll continue in exactly that same course. We'll no longer be subject to the passions and the appetites of the flesh. We will have passed successfully the tests of this mortal probation and in due course we'll get the fulness of our Father's kingdom—and that means eternal life in his everlasting presence."[5]

Few of those who have embraced the ways of the world will enter the gate and traverse the strait and narrow path. Many of our Father's children, however, even "an innumerable company" of the just (see D&C 138:12; see also 76:67), will come out of the world, enter the gate, get onto the path, and continue faithful until they reach the tree whose fruit is the most desirable of all things and the most joyous to the soul.

The Lord has declared anew in our dispensation that "he who doeth the works of righteousness shall receive his reward, even peace in this world, and eternal life in the world to come" (D&C 59:23). Isaiah had written some twenty-six hundred years earlier, "And the work of righteousness shall be peace; and the effect of righteousness quietness and assurance for ever" (Isaiah 32:17). Those in this life who conduct themselves with fidelity and devotion to God and his laws will eventually know that peace "which passeth all understanding" (Philippians 4:7), the calming but powerful assurance that one has successfully met the challenges of mortality. These are they who have lived by every word of God and are willing to serve the Lord at all hazards. They have made their calling and election sure.[6] For such persons, the day of judgment has been advanced, and the blessings associated with the glories of the celestial kingdom are assured. They receive what the Prophet Joseph called "the more sure word of prophecy," which, he explained, "means a man's knowing that he is sealed up unto eternal life, by revelation and the spirit of prophecy, through the power of the Holy Priesthood. It is impossible for a man to be saved in ignorance" (D&C 131:5–6). Though it is true, as President Marion G. Romney observed, that "the fulness of eternal life is not attainable in mortality, . . . the peace which is its harbinger and which comes as a result of making one's calling and election sure is attainable in this life."[7]

Latter-day Saints who have received the ordinances of salvation—including the blessings of the temple endowment and eternal marriage—may thus press forward in the work of the Lord and with quiet dignity and patient maturity seek to be worthy of gaining the certain assurance of salvation before the end of their mortal lives. Should one not formally receive that assurance in this life, however, one has the scriptural promise that faithfully

enduring to the end—that is, keeping the covenants and commandments from baptism to the end of one's life (see Mosiah
18:8–9)—brings the promise of eternal life, whether that promise be received here or hereafter (see D&C 14:7; 53:7; 2 Nephi
31:20; Mosiah 5:15). "But blessed are they who are faithful and
endure, *whether in life or in death,* for they shall inherit eternal
life" (D&C 50:5; emphasis added).

Life in the highest heaven hereafter is a reality and a possibility, a goal within the reach of every one of us. That knowledge
provides focus and direction to our actions. *Salvation, eternal life,
eternal lives, exaltation*—all expressions connoting the glories of
the celestial kingdom and a life that is similar to God's own life—
represent the grand purpose of our sojourn on this earth and the
reason we do what we do in the Church and in the home. To
those who have developed the precious faith of the ancients (see
2 Peter 1:1) come the blessings enjoyed by the ancients: the fulness of the glory of the Father and a continuation of the family
unit forever and ever.

Chapter 8

THE BEGINNING OF ETERNITY

I have reflected many times on the horrendous decision that Abraham, the father of the faithful, faced when Jehovah commanded him to sacrifice his son, his covenant son, the son through whom the promises of God and the hopes of Abraham and Sarah were to be realized. Such reflections have especially haunted me since I first became a father myself in 1972. I have wrestled with the following questions: Would I have sufficient integrity to obey the Lord in the face of what many would consider to be an absurd requirement? Is there something in life that matters more to me than God? Does my love for my family surpass my devotion to the Almighty? Haunting questions, these.

I have thought about pioneer mothers who laid their infant in a shallow grave and moved on to a distant Zion. Much less dramatically, I have thought of a familiar scene of young mothers caring for the needs of multiple children, day after day. I can envision families gathered for family home evening, Mom and Dad trying desperately to separate the fighting boys, pleading with the uninterested teenagers to stay just a few minutes more, hoping against hope that amid the chaos and disruption a spark of inspiration might be felt by their children.

As I have pondered such scenarios, I have wondered how true and tried souls like Abraham could do it, how they could do what seemed to be the unthinkable. How do young mothers keep going, especially when they are so weary? How can they face what seems like an eternal grind, over and over, again and again? How can parents have prayer or read scriptures or convene family home evening when at the moment the meeting seems to be anything but inspiring?

In wrestling with such hard questions, I have been reminded of the apostle Paul's "who's who of faith," a recitation of many of the men and women through the ages who demonstrated saving faith in the God of their fathers and mothers. Paul summarized: "These all died in faith, not having received the promises, *but having seen them afar off, and were persuaded of them, and embraced them*, and confessed that they were strangers and pilgrims on the earth" (Hebrews 11:13; emphasis added).

Alma the Younger inquired of the Saints in Zarahemla: "Do you look forward *with an eye of faith*, and view this mortal body raised in immortality, and this corruption raised in incorruption, to stand before God to be judged according to the deeds which have been done in the mortal body?" (Alma 5:15; emphasis added). That same Alma warned the Zoramites that if they did not "nourish the word, *looking forward with an eye of faith* to the fruit thereof, ye can never pluck of the fruit of the tree of life" (Alma 32:40; emphasis added). Finally, in what we might call Moroni's own "who's who of faith," he pointed out, "There were many whose faith was so exceedingly strong, even before Christ came, who could not be kept from within the veil, but truly *saw with their eyes the things which they had* [previously] *beheld with an eye of faith*, and they were glad" (Ether 12:19; emphasis added).

Seeing things with an eye of faith is looking out and beyond to the distant scene, viewing today's often repetitious and some-times monotonous comings and goings with an eye toward eter-nity. It is to see beyond the moment, to acquire a portion of God's perspective, to realize that "out of small things proceedeth that which is great" (D&C 64:33). Young students of the gospel may little appreciate that the investment every day of even a short time spent pondering the scriptures—a spiritual discipline conducted regularly and consistently with devotion and hope—will gradually and almost imperceptibly bring about a mighty change. Such budding Saints come to live their lives by divine principle and precept, for they have been drenched in the learn-ing and language and logic of scripture, schooled subtly in the wisdom of heaven. It is through pursuing our daily walk and talk with an eye of faith, with an eye toward the glories of the future, that we make proper preparation for our Lord's return and his reign on earth.

We have now spoken at some length about the second com-ing of Jesus Christ to earth; the transformation of this fallen orb into a paradisiacal abode of the faithful; daily life and the work to be accomplished during that glorious period of peace and joy the scriptures call the Millennium; the rise of the body and its reuniting with the spirit in resurrection, thus bringing to pass the immortality of the soul; the time of judgment, when every person who has lived on this planet will render an accounting for his or her earthly stewardship; and the kingdoms of glory that await each of us after resurrection and judgment.

We have also looked carefully at many of the details and pro-phetic particulars of the days that lie ahead. Some of these mat-ters are *nice* to know, others are matters we really *should* know, and a few are matters we *must* know. It's nice to be able to speak intelligently of the visits the Savior will make to the earth before his coming in glory. A serious student of the scriptures really should know what kinds of persons will inherit the celestial, terrestrial, and telestial kingdoms of glory. But everyone *must* know, whether in this life or in the life to come, that Jesus Christ is the Son of the Living God; that he suffered and bled and died in Gethsemane and on Golgotha as a substitutionary offering for all of the children of God; that he rose from the dead in glorious immortality; that because of his resurrection, we too have the hope of that fulness of joy that comes with the inseparable union of body and spirit; and that exaltation and eternal life come in and through his atoning sacrifice and in no other way. Salvation is in Christ! That is the truth of truths, the doctrine of doctrines, the message of messages.

Surely all true Christians want to know everything they can about the Redeemer, the Author and Finisher of their faith. They yearn both to know about him and to know him. The scriptures declare that a deeply significant title and role of our Lord and Master is the Millennial Messiah—the One who will come again, this time in majesty and might and glory, this time to cleanse the earth of wickedness, this time to bring in an era of peace and goodwill and transcendent knowledge. Although some of the details we have considered may not be immediately essential to our salvation, they are details that relate and pertain to him who has bought us with his blood and has prepared a mansion for us in the kingdoms that await us. To know of what the scriptures and latter-day prophets teach about life in the Millennium is to know what it will be like to live and move and have our being on an earth where Jesus the Messiah reigns as King of kings and Lord of lords. It is to gain something of a feeling—if only a sweet foretaste—for how glorious it will be on the paradisiacal earth to hear him preach his gospel, see him direct his earthly Church and kingdom, and thereby bless his people with his personal presence.

To be sure, trying times await the Saints of God, and there are, as President Heber C. Kimball pointed out, "many close places through which [this Church] will have to pass before the work of God is crowned with victory. To meet the difficulties that are coming, it will be necessary for you to have a knowledge of the truth of this work for yourselves. The difficulties will be of such a character that the man or woman who does not possess this personal knowledge or witness will fall. . . . The time will come when no man nor woman will be able to endure on borrowed light. Each will have to be guided by the light within himself. If you do not have it, how can you stand?"[1]

Nonetheless, we look to the future with an eye of faith, with a perspective informed by scripture and an outlook sustained by doctrinal optimism and gospel gladness. President Howard W. Hunter pointed out that "Jesus taught his disciples to watch and pray; however, he taught them that prayerful watching does not require sleepless anxiety and preoccupation with the future, but rather the quiet, steady attention to present duties."[2] His prophetic successor, President Gordon B. Hinckley, advised that "we need not wait . . . for that millennial morning. We can improve today without waiting for tomorrow. We can alter circumstances ourselves, without waiting for others. We can hold back the forces that debilitate and weaken us. We can strengthen the forces that will improve the world."[3]

Ours is not a religion of doom and gloom but rather a way of life that evermore points us toward the One who beckons: "These things I have spoken unto you, that in me ye might have peace. In the world ye shall have tribulation: but be of good cheer; I have overcome the world" (John 16:33). "Wherefore," the Lord declared in modern revelation, "fear not even unto death; for in this world your joy is not full, but in me your joy is full." We are thus charged to "seek the face of the Lord always, that in patience ye may possess your souls, and ye shall have eternal life" (D&C 101:36, 38).

In speaking of the Savior's second coming and of life in the Millennium, President Hinckley declared: "It will be a time of great and terrible fears, of cataclysmic upheavals of nature, of weeping and wailing, of repentance too late, and of crying out unto the Lord for mercy. But for those who in that judgment are found acceptable, it will be a day for thanksgiving, for the Lord shall come with his angels, and the apostles who were with him in life, and those who have been resurrected. Further, the graves of the righteous will be opened and they shall come forth. Then will begin the great Millennium, a period of a thousand years when Satan shall be bound and the Lord shall reign over his people. Can you imagine the wonder and the beauty of that era when the adversary shall not have influence? Think of his pull upon you now and reflect on the peace of that time when you will be free from such influence. There will be quiet and goodness where now there is contention and evil."[4] President Lorenzo Snow stated: "Jesus will come by and by, and appear in our midst, as He appeared in the day when upon the earth among the Jews, and He will eat and drink with us and talk to us, and explain the mysteries of the Kingdom, and tell us things that are not lawful to talk about now."[5] And President Spencer W. Kimball offered wise counsel on how to pursue our preparation: "When Satan is bound in a single home—when Satan is bound in a single life— the Millennium has already begun in that home, in that life."[6]

We have hope. We have rejoicing. God is in his heaven. The Church of Jesus Christ of Latter-day Saints is in the line of its duty: it is preparing a people for the second coming of the Son of Man. It is in extremely capable hands, for it is guided by prophets, seers, and revelators, men ordained and empowered to see afar off, to view the distant scene without fear or anxiety. This is the work of God, and our Savior is the Head. If it were the work of a man it would fail, but it is the Church of the Lord Jesus Christ, and he does not fail. As individuals and as the people of the covenant, we "press toward the mark for the prize of the high calling of God in Christ Jesus" (Philippians 3:14), "being confident of this very thing, that he which hath begun a good work in [us] will perform it [accomplish or complete it] until the day of Jesus Christ" (Philippians 1:6). With such an assurance, our souls are at peace.

NOTES

PREFACE

1. "Come, Let Us Anew," *Hymns,* no. 217.
2. "Jehovah, Lord of Heaven and Earth," *Hymns,* no. 269.
3. Packer, *Mine Errand from the Lord,* 399–400.
4. Packer, *Mine Errand from the Lord,* 400.

CHAPTER 1: THE END OF TIME

1. Smith, *History of the Church,* 1:338; emphasis added.

CHAPTER 2: THE SAVIOR'S PRELIMINARY APPEARANCES

1. McConkie, *Millennial Messiah,* 577–78.
2. Pratt, *Journal of Discourses,* 15:365–66.
3. Penrose, "Second Advent," *Millennial Star* 21 (10 Sept. 1859): 582–83.
4. Smith, *History of the Church,* 3:386–87.
5. Smith, *Progress of Man,* 481–82; see also Smith, *Way to Perfection,* 288–91; McConkie, *Millennial Messiah,* 582–84.
6. Orson Pratt, *Journal of Discourses,* 17:186.
7. See McConkie, *Doctrinal New Testament Commentary,* 3:509; *Millennial Messiah,* 390.
8. Hinckley, "As One Who Loves the Prophet," in Black and Tate, *Joseph Smith,* 2–3.

CHAPTER 3: JESUS CHRIST COMES IN GLORY

1. Pratt, *Journal of Discourses,* 16:319.

2. Ballard, "When Shall These Things Be?" in *BYU Speeches*, 186; emphasis added.

3. Smith, "Correspondence," *Times and Seasons* 4, no. 8 (1 Mar. 1843): 113; emphasis added.

4. Smith, *Signs of the Times*, 41.

5. Smith, *History of the Church*, 5:387, 392, 403.

6. Maxwell, *Even As I Am*, 120.

7. Smith, *Signs of the Times*, 42.

8. See McConkie, *Millennial Messiah*, 26–27, 405.

9. *Teachings of Gordon B. Hinckley*, 577.

CHAPTER 4: A THOUSAND YEARS OF PEACE AND GLORY

1. Maxwell, *Wherefore, Ye Must Press Forward*, 5.

2. Holland, *Christ and the New Covenant*, 87.

3. Pratt, *Journal of Discourses*, 16:319.

4. *Teachings of Ezra Taft Benson*, 18.

5. Smith, *History of the Church*, 4:425.

6. Pratt, *Journal of Discourses*, 14:242–43; 16:325; 18:25.

7. Romney, "The Light Shineth," *Ensign*, Dec. 1971, 75.

8. Smith, *History of the Church*, 5:423–24.

9. Maxwell, *Wonderful Flood of Light*, 18.

10. Smith, *History of the Church*, 4:540.

11. Smith, *History of the Church*, 5:423.

12. Young, *Journal of Discourses*, 13:329.

13. Woodruff, *Journal of Discourses*, 13:327.

14. Smith, "Redemption beyond the Grave," *Improvement Era* 5 (Dec. 1901): 146–47.

15. Young, *Journal of Discourses*, 3:372.

16. Young, *Journal of Discourses*, 11:275.

17. Young, *Journal of Discourses*, 2:316.

18. Young, *Journal of Discourses*, 12:274.

19. Smith, *Doctrines of Salvation*, 3:64.

20. See Smith, *Doctrines of Salvation*, 3:63–64; Smith, *Teachings of the Prophet Joseph Smith*, 268–69n2.

21. Smith, *History of the Church*, 5:212.

22. Cannon, *Gospel Truth*, 70; emphasis added.

23. Oaks, *With Full Purpose of Heart*, 35; emphasis added.

24. Holland, *Christ and the New Covenant*, 296–97.

25. "The Day Dawn Is Breaking," *Hymns*, no. 52.

26. Smith, *History of the Church*, 3:380.

27. Smith, *History of the Church*, 5:212.

28. See Smith, *Words of Joseph Smith*, 14–15.

29. Cannon, *Gospel Truth*, 71.

30. Cannon, *Journal of Discourses*, 16:120.

31. Pratt, *Journal of Discourses*, 16:322; see also Smith, *Doctrines of Salvation*, 2:56–57.

32. See McConkie, *New Witness*, 652.

33. Smith, *History of the Church*, 5:298.

CHAPTER 5: BEING RAISED FROM THE DEAD

1. See Smith, *History of the Church*, 5:388.

2. Smith, *History of the Church*, 2:18.

3. Smith, *History of the Church*, 4:555.

4. Smith, *Gospel Doctrine*, 23.

5. Smith, *History of the Church*, 5:339.

6. Young, "The Resurrection," *Elders' Journal* 1 (July 1904): 153.

7. Smith, *Gospel Doctrine*, 25.

8. McConkie, *Promised Messiah*, 215–16; emphasis added.

9. McConkie, *Millennial Messiah*, 520; emphasis added.

10. Young, *Journal of Discourses*, 15:137.

11. Young, *Journal of Discourses*, 9:140.

12. Snow, *Journal of Discourses*, 25:34.

13. Pratt, *Masterful Discourses and Writings*, 62–63; emphasis added.

14. Smith, *History of the Church*, 6:50.

15. Smith, *History of the Church*, 5:362.

16. Smith, *History of the Church*, 5:362.

CHAPTER 6: MANY MANSIONS OF THE FATHER

1. Smith, *History of the Church*, 1:238.

2. Andrus and Andrus, *They Knew the Prophet*, 67–68.

3. Smith, *History of the Church*, 5:402.

4. Smith, "Vision," *Times and Seasons* 4, no. 6 (1 Feb. 1843): 82–83, stanzas 18–20.

5. Nelson, *Perfection Pending*, 167.

6. Smith, *History of the Church*, 6:314.

7. Smith, *History of the Church*, 6:314–15.

8. Smith, *History of the Church*, 1:366.

9. Smith, "Vision," *Times and Seasons* 4, no. 6 (1 Feb. 1843): 84, stanza 43.

10. See Smith, *Doctrines of Salvation*, 2:42; *Man, His Origin and Destiny*, 272; *Way to Perfection*, 208.

11. See McConkie, *Doctrinal New Testament Commentary*, 2:472, 474–75, 491.

12. Young, *Journal of Discourses*, 8:154.

13. Smith, *History of the Church*, 5:555.

14. Smith, "Vision," *Times and Seasons* 4, no. 6 (1 Feb. 1843): 84, stanza 57.

15. Smith, "Vision," *Times and Seasons* 4, no. 6 (1 Feb. 1843): 85, stanzas 70–71.

16. Ballard, *Crusader for Righteousness*, 224–25.

17. Smith, *Doctrines of Salvation*, 2:32; emphasis in original.

18. Kimball, *Miracle of Forgiveness*, 243–44.

19. Penrose, "Mormon" Doctrine, 72, 74, 75; emphasis added.

20. Smith, *History of the Church*, 5:391.

21. Wilkinson, *A Life God Rewards*, 23, 25, 73.

22. MacArthur, cited in Wilkinson, *A Life God Rewards*, 120.

23. Augustine, *City of God*, 779; emphasis added.

24. Edwards, cited in Wilkinson, *A Life God Rewards*, 119; emphasis added. Edwards's use of the word *designed* may well reflect his Calvinistic belief in predestination.

25. Wesley, cited in Wilkinson, *A Life God Rewards*, 120–21.

26. Smith, *History of the Church*, 1:252–53.

27. Smith, *History of the Church*, 6:365.

CHAPTER 7: SALVATION, EXALTATION, AND ETERNAL LIFE

1. *Lectures on Faith*, 76.

2. Smith, *History of the Church*, 5:387.

3. McConkie, *Promised Messiah*, 129; compare 306; see also McConkie, *New Witness*, 144–54.

4. Smith, *History of the Church*, 4:360; Smith, *Doctrines of Salvation*, 1:61.

5. McConkie, "Jesus Christ and Him Crucified," 398, 400–401.

6. Smith, *History of the Church*, 3:380–81.

7. Romney, Conference Report, Oct. 1965, 20.

CHAPTER 8: THE BEGINNING OF ETERNITY

1. Whitney, *Life of Heber C. Kimball*, 446, 449–50.

2. *Teachings of Howard W. Hunter*, 201.
3. Hinckley, *Be Thou an Example*, 16.
4. *Teachings of Gordon B. Hinckley*, 576.
5. *Lorenzo Snow* [manual], 282.
6. *Teachings of Spencer W. Kimball*, 172.

GLOSSARY

Adam. Adam is the father of the human family, the first mortal on earth, and the one designated in scripture as the Ancient of Days (Daniel 7:22; D&C 27:11). He will preside at the Council of Adam-ondi-Ahman, under the direction of Jesus Christ. Adam also holds, under the Lord's direction, the keys associated with the resurrection (D&C 29:26; 78:16).

Adam-ondi-Ahman. The site of one of the Savior's preliminary appearances prior to his coming in glory, Adam-ondi-Ahman is the place where all those who have held the keys of the priesthood in the various dispensations will give an accounting to Adam (D&C 116:1). As the head of the human family, Adam will then account to Jesus Christ, whose right it is to reign forevermore as King of kings and Lord of lords (D&C 58:22).

Antichrist. An antichrist is one who denies, defies, strives to oppose, and fights against the Lord Jesus and the plan of redemption. This may be a person, an organization, or a false point of view.

Apocalypse. The word *apocalypse* means "uncovering, unveiling, revealing." Characteristics of apocalyptic writing include symbolic numbers, strange creatures, astral phenomena (signs in the heavens), cosmic dualism (day and night, black and white, good and evil, God and Satan), and an overriding message to hold on. Satan may seem to be in charge for the time being, but the day is not far distant when the God of heaven will intervene in history, bring an end to evil, and initiate an era of righteousness. Although apocalyptic writings and themes are found in various books of scripture

(Ezekiel; Daniel; Matthew 24; Mark 13; 1 Nephi 13–14), the Apocalypse, or the Revelation, of John the Beloved is the most comprehensive example of this prophetic genre.

Armageddon. Although the word *Armageddon* refers specifically to the hills of Megiddo and a battle in northern Israel that will take place just before our Lord's coming in glory, the name Armageddon may also describe the continuing worldwide battle between good and evil. On one side are the forces of Satan, described as the great and abominable church (2 Nephi 6:12; D&C 29:21) or mother of harlots (Revelation 13:34). On the other side are the forces of righteousness, the covenant people of the Lord (Acts 3:25; 1 Nephi 14:14) or the Church of the Lamb of God (1 Nephi 14:10, 12, 14).

Babylon. Ancient Babylon was a powerful nation that proved to be a formidable, almost perennial, foe to the children of Israel. Over time, the word *Babylon* came to mean evil influences and diabolical forces arrayed against the people of God (1 Peter 5:13; Revelation 14:8; 17:5; 18:2; D&C 1:16; 35:11; 64:24; 86:3; 133:5, 7, 14).

Bridegroom. Jesus Christ is described in metaphoric terms as the Bridegroom (D&C 65:3) and the people of his Church are the bride (D&C 109:73–74). Just as in ancient times the bridegroom would journey with the wedding party to the home of his intended bride to convey her to the wedding, even so will the Lord Jesus Christ return to earth with hosts of the righteous dead to receive his Church and kingdom on earth. The wedding feast is a reunion between the people of the covenant and the Mediator of that covenant.

Celestial kingdom. The celestial kingdom is the highest heaven, the noblest and grandest attainment hereafter to which the children of God can aspire. It will be inhabited by those who have the testimony of Jesus and have received the covenant gospel; have entered into the Lord's Church and kingdom by subscribing to the first principles and ordinances of the gospel; have sought to keep the commandments of God; have overcome the world through their faith in Jesus Christ; have been sealed by the Holy Spirit of Promise; have been received into the Church of the Firstborn; have become kings and queens, priests and priestesses unto God; and who have become gods, even the sons and daughters of God (D&C 76:51–58). Additional inhabitants will be those who did not have the opportunity to receive the fulness of the gospel in this life but who would have received it had they had that opportunity, including children who died before the age of accountability (D&C 137:7–10). This earth, in its sanctified and glorified state, will become the celestial kingdom (D&C 88:15–20; 130:9).

Church of the Firstborn. The Church of the Firstborn is made up of those who qualify for eternal life. Whereas baptism is the means by which individuals are born again and received into the family of the Lord Jesus Christ, temple sealing and subsequent faithfulness to temple covenants are the means by which members of the Church become the sons and daughters of God the Father. They thereby become joint heirs, or coinheritors with Christ, to all the Father has (D&C 76:54–59, 71, 94–95). They qualify to inherit with Christ, who is the natural firstborn, as though they themselves were the firstborn (D&C 93:21–22).

Dispensation of the fulness of times. A dispensation is a period of time during which the fulness of the gospel, including the holy priesthood and the knowledge of God's plan of salvation, are revealed and conferred through prophets to the children of the Father. We live now in the dispensation of the fulness of times, which is the last, or final, dispensation during the period of the earth's temporal continuance (D&C 27:13; 110:16). There will never again be a complete apostasy of the Lord's Church. This final dispensation is, as it were, the grand ocean of truth and power into which all of the streams and rivers of past dispensations now flow (D&C 121:26–32).

Elias. As described in latter-day revelation, Elias signifies a messenger or a forerunner, one who goes before and prepares the way. Just as John the Baptist prepared the way for the mortal Messiah and was thus an Elias in the meridian dispensation, even so Joseph Smith has prepared the way for the Savior's second coming and is an Elias in this final dispensation. Similarly, Elias can signify multiple messengers or angels. Moroni, for example, was the fulfillment of the prophecy of John concerning another angel flying through the midst of heaven having the everlasting gospel (Revelation 14:6–7); so also were John the Baptist, Peter, James, John, Moses, Elijah, Michael, Raphael, and hosts of other heavenly ministrants (D&C 27:6–13; 128:21).

End of the earth. The end of the earth comes at the end of the thousand years we know as the Millennium (D&C 38:5; 43:31; 88:101;

Joseph Smith–Matthew 1:55). It is then that this planet will be celestialized.

End of the world. The end of the world is the destruction of the wicked, the end of worldliness, that will happen at the time of the Savior's coming in glory, when he cleanses the earth by fire (Joseph Smith–Matthew 1:4, 31; 2 Nephi 30:10; Jacob 6:3).

Endure to the end. To endure to the end is to keep our covenants until we have finished our work here on the earth—until we die. It is to leave this earth temple worthy, active, and faithful in the Church. Those who endure to the end will receive eternal life (1 Nephi 13:37; 22:31; 2 Nephi 31:15; 3 Nephi 27:6; D&C 6:13; 14:7; 18:22; 50:5; 101:35).

Eternal life. Eternal life is God's life, salvation in the highest degree of the celestial kingdom, a life reserved for those who receive the fulness of the power and glory of the Father.

Eternal lives. To have eternal lives is to have eternal life and to qualify for that life hereafter in which the family unit continues everlastingly (D&C 132:19, 24).

Eternal progression. The plan by which individuals grow and develop from the time of their birth as spirits until the time they are glorified in the resurrection is often referred to as eternal progression. It is a system of faith that enables the children of God to gradually acquire the fruit of the Spirit (Galatians 5:22–25); to gain the mind of Christ (1 Corinthians 2:16); to come to embody and reflect charity, or the pure love of Christ (Moroni 7:47–48); and to see God as he is, for they will have become like him (1 John 3:1–3).

Exaltation. To receive exaltation is to receive eternal life. In addition, it is to qualify for life with God and with our family everlastingly. While salvation pertains to individuals, exaltation is a family affair.

False Christs. Other than those few deluded individuals who suppose they are Jesus or have some unnatural messiah complex, false Christs are false systems of salvation, false teachings or practices or lifestyles that lead one away from "peace in this world, and eternal life in the world to come" (D&C 59:23).

False prophets. False prophets are false purveyors of information, blind guides (Matthew 23:16), or those who proselytize the unwary to accept the precepts of men.

Fire and brimstone. Joseph Smith spoke of the expression "fire and brimstone" as a metaphor. He taught that the "torment of disappointment in the mind of man"—the realization of what we could have done and who we could have become and yet did not—"is as exquisite as a lake burning with fire and brimstone" (*Joseph Smith* [manual], 224).

Gathering of Israel. Individuals and whole nations are gathered when they accept the true Messiah, his gospel, his church, and his doctrine and congregate with the faithful (1 Nephi 15:13–16; 2 Nephi 6:8–11; 9:1–2; 10:3–7). One of the signs of the times is that the children of Israel will begin to be gathered into the Church and kingdom of God in greater and greater numbers in the time preparatory to the ushering in of the Millennium. The gathering is accomplished through missionary work, as "one of a city, and two of a family" (Jeremiah 3:14) are taught the principles of the restored gospel and receive baptism and confirmation and the blessings of the temple at the hands of authorized administrators. Persons participate in the final phase of the gathering as they receive the covenants and ordinances of the temple (*Joseph Smith* [manual], 416–17). The great day of the gathering is millennial.

Gentile. In one sense, a person is a Gentile who is not a descendant of Abraham or one of the twelve sons of Jacob. In a broader, scriptural sense, a Gentile is someone from "the nations," meaning a nation or country outside the Holy Land (1 Nephi 22:6–11; 2 Nephi 30:4; 33:8). In that sense, most Latter-day Saints are Israelite by descent but Gentile by culture or nation (1 Nephi 22:7; D&C 109:60).

Gentiles, times of the. Jesus taught that the first shall be last and the last shall be first (Matthew 19:30; 20:16; 1 Nephi 13:42; Jacob 5:63). This teaching has to do with the order in which the gospel is presented to the children of men. In the meridian of time, the gospel went first to the Jews and then to the Gentiles (Matthew 10:5–6; 15:24). In our day, the gospel was restored in a great Gentile nation (1 Nephi 22:7) and will eventually go to all the children of Israel. The times of the Gentiles is that day when the gospel of Jesus Christ comes first to and through those denominated as Gentiles, meaning cultural Gentiles. The fulness of the times of the Gentiles is that time when the Gentiles will have rejected and sinned against the fulness of the gospel and thus disqualified themselves for its benefits and blessings. The gospel will then be taken from the Gentiles and given to the Jews (see, for example, 3 Nephi 16:10–11; D&C 45:24–25).

Godhood. One of the grand and transcendent purposes of the gospel
of Jesus Christ is to sanctify and transform the children of God, to
prepare them not only to dwell with God hereafter but also to be
like him. To be like God is to be Christlike, to embody the fruit of
the Spirit (Galatians 5:22–25), and to live and interact as did our
Master, the prototype of all saved beings, when he dwelt on earth.
To attain godhood is to become perfect (whole, complete, mature;
Matthew 5:48*b*) in and through Christ (Moroni 10:32); to become
a joint heir with Christ (Romans 8:14–18; D&C 76:68); to be a
partaker of the divine nature (2 Peter 1:4); and to become, by spiritual regeneration, the son or daughter of God. These are they who
are gods (D&C 76:58).

Gog and Magog, battle of. The final great battle between the forces
of evil and the forces of good, between Satan and God, between
Lucifer and Michael, is called the battle of Gog and Magog. It takes
place at the end of the Millennium (*History of the Church*, 5:298).
After Satan is dismissed and banished from earth forevermore
(Revelation 20:7–10), the earth will be sanctified and become the
celestial kingdom.

Great and abominable church. The great and abominable church
(1 Nephi 13:5), the church of the devil or the whore of all the
earth (1 Nephi 14:10), or the mother of harlots (1 Nephi 13:34) is
that organization of evil, that consortium of corruption, that fights
against Zion, denies and defies the work of the Lord and even the
Lord himself (2 Nephi 10:16). It is any organization—social, eco-
nomic, political, fraternal, philosophical, or religious—that either
secretly or openly opposes righteousness in the earth and the establishment of the kingdom of God. Eventually those persons and
organizations who make up the church of the devil will turn upon
themselves, and Babylon will fall (Revelation 18; 1 Nephi 22:13–
14, 22–23).

Heaven. The traditional Christian world holds that there are only two
possible states or conditions a person will enjoy when he or she
leaves this life: heaven or hell. But Jesus explained that "in my
Father's house are many mansions" (John 14:2). The apostle Paul
taught that there are different types of bodies in the resurrection,
dependent upon what level of righteousness a person chose in mortality to pursue (JST, 1 Corinthians 15:40–42). The Prophet Joseph
Smith learned by vision (D&C 76) that there are more heavens

than one hereafter—celestial, terrestrial, and telestial. With the exception of those who defect to perdition, God will save all his children in a kingdom of glory (D&C 76:40–43).

Hell. At the moment individuals breathe their last, they enter the postmortal spirit world. There each experiences a partial judgment and takes up residence either in paradise (the abode of the righteous; Alma 40:12) or in what the scriptures call hell, outer darkness, or spirit prison (the abode of the wicked, as well as those who have yet to learn of the gospel; 1 Peter 3:18–20; 4:6; 2 Nephi 9:10–12; Alma 40:13–14). At the time of the second, or last, resurrection (the resurrection of telestial persons and sons of perdition) the spirit world is emptied (2 Nephi 9:12), and all are resurrected (Alma 11:41). Except for the sons of perdition, those who inherit an eternal outer darkness (D&C 76:33, 37–38), hell will be no more.

Holy Spirit of Promise. The Holy Spirit of Promise is the Holy Ghost, the Holy Spirit promised to the Saints. This third member of the Godhead is a comforter, a teacher, a testifier, a sanctifier, and a sealer. Because he knows all things (D&C 42:17; Moses 6:61), the Comforter is able to search the minds and hearts of all people and determine those who have obeyed the truth and sought after goodness and righteousness. The Spirit certifies that such a person is a just man or woman and worthy of eternal life. He ratifies, or approves, all covenants and ordinances a person has received (baptism, confirmation, ordination for men, endowment, and sealing) and places an eternal stamp upon that life. It may then be said that this person has been sealed by the Holy Spirit of Promise. If a worthy couple enters the house of the Lord, participates in a celestial marriage, and keeps their covenants until the end of their lives, that union is sealed by the Holy Spirit of Promise, and they will enjoy the blessings of exaltation.

Immortality. To receive immortality is to live forever. The doctrines of the Restoration set forth the profound truth that we are eternal beings, that we have always lived, that we already, in that sense, possess immortality. What the Savior makes available to us is resurrected, glorified immortality in the presence of God and the Lamb.

Joint heirs with Christ. Those who receive the gospel covenant with its attendant ordinances become the sons and daughters of the Lord Jesus Christ by adoption. Those who thereafter receive the ordinances of the temple and keep their covenants become the sons and daughters of God, meaning the Father (Mosiah 27:25; D&C 11:30; 76:58; Moses 7:1). They become joint heirs, or co-inheritors, with Jesus Christ to all the Father has (Romans 8:17; D&C 76:55).

Judgment Day. The Saints of God pass through a series of judgments throughout their lives. At the time of death, individuals undergo a partial judgment (Alma 40:11–13) and are assigned to either paradise or hell, which is outer darkness (Alma 40:11–13). When individuals are resurrected, they experience a kind of judgment in being raised with a body adapted to the kingdom of glory each will inherit—celestial, terrestrial, or telestial (D&C 76:28–31). The Final Judgment, which Christians refer to as Judgment Day, comes after the second, or last, resurrection.

Lost tribes of Israel. The ten northern tribes of Israel were scattered throughout the nations after the Assyrian captivity in 721 B.C. and became known as the lost tribes of Israel (1 Nephi 22:3–4). Through the generations that followed, persons and groups who chose to follow Jehovah and associate with the people of the covenant were gathered, first spiritually (to the Lord and his gospel) and then temporally (to the lands of their inheritance). As time moves on toward the day when Jesus Christ will return in glory, the missionary efforts of The Church of Jesus Christ of Latter-day Saints will intensify, and members of the house of Israel whose lineal descent is from those tribes who were once a part of the northern tribes will come into the Church through baptism, gather with the Saints in the congregations where they reside, receive the ordinances of the temple, endure faithfully to the end of their lives, and thereby qualify for eternal life. The gathering of the ten tribes is largely a millennial endeavor (2 Nephi 30:7–15; 3 Nephi 21:25–26).

Millennium. When Jesus Christ returns in power and glory, the Millennium begins (D&C 29:11). It will be a thousand years of peace and rest, joy and happiness, and freedom from the woes and waywardness of our present telestial world. The earth and the mortals who inhabit it will be raised to a terrestrial level of glory. The Millennium will be brought in by the cleansing and renovating power of the Savior, and it will be maintained by the righteousness of the people (1 Nephi 22:15, 26).

Mountain of the Lord's house. A scriptural phrase that refers to the connecting links between God and man, the mountain of the Lord's house represents the high and holy places we know as temples, or houses of the Lord (Isaiah 2:2–3; compare D&C 84:2–4). Temples link time and eternity, past, present, and future, the living and the dead, husbands and wives, parents and children, and each individual to Christ.

A new heaven and a new earth. When Jesus returns in glory, the earth and its heavenly surroundings will be "renewed and receive [their] paradisiacal glory" (Articles of Faith 1:10). That is, it will be raised to a terrestrial glory. At the end of the Millennium, the earth will be raised to a celestial glory and thus be prepared for those who will receive eternal life and exaltation to inhabit it (D&C 56:18–20). And so, once again, there will be a new heaven and a new earth (Isaiah 65:17; Revelation 21:1; D&C 29:23).

Olivet prophecy. During the last week of his mortal life, the Savior took his apostles to the Mount of Olives and there set forth many of what we know as the signs of the times—the events leading up to his coming in glory: false Christs, false prophets, wars and rumors of wars, men's hearts failing them, gospel preached to all the world, and so forth. Both Matthew 24 and Mark 13 present these signs in an orderly fashion. Joseph Smith's translation of Matthew 24 (which is reflected exactly in JST, Mark 13) is more comprehensive, more systematic, and far more insightful than those in other versions of the Bible, including the King James Version. Joseph Smith's translation of these chapters may well be our most complete prophetic expression of what lies ahead.

One hundred forty-four thousand. Modern revelation provides insight into the rather enigmatic group referred to in chapters 7 and 14 of John's Revelation. These one hundred forty-four thousand persons are high priests after the holy order of God, men who have the assignment to "bring as many as will come to the church of the Firstborn" (D&C 77:11). Their role is to make available to individuals throughout the earth the fulness of the blessings of the priesthood, thereby sealing up unto eternal life the Saints of the Most High. Perhaps more than anything else, this number is a prophetic statement that because in that day temples will dot the earth, all the blessings of those temples will be available to an ever-expanding number of God's children.

Outer darkness. See *Hell* in this glossary.

Paradise. See *Hell* in this glossary.

Paradisiacal glory. See *A new heaven and a new earth* in this glossary.

Perdition, son of. Joseph Smith explained that in order for a person to commit the unpardonable sin and thereby become a son of perdition, that person must "receive the Holy Ghost, have the heavens opened . . . , know God, and then sin against Him" (*History of the Church*, 6:314). Sons of perdition are persons who have enjoyed an unusual outpouring of spiritual light and understanding and then choose to deny the faith and fight the work of the Lord. They blaspheme against the Holy Ghost (Matthew 12:31–32) and shed anew the innocent blood of Christ (Hebrews 6:4–6; 10:26–29; D&C 76:28–39; 132:27). Sons of perdition are the only ones who will be subject to the second, or final, spiritual death (D&C 76:36–39; 132:27).

Priesthood, fulness of. The fulness of the blessings of the priesthood are to be had only through the covenants and ordinances of the temple (D&C 124:48). Those who receive the fulness of the priesthood are kings and queens, priests and priestesses, unto God in the house of Israel (Revelation 1:6; D&C 76:56; *Joseph Smith* [manual], 109).

The rest of the Lord. The scriptures speak often of how the faithful may enter into the rest of God (Alma 12:34; 13:12). Entering into his rest takes place when a person is living the gospel and gains the peace associated with a settled conviction of the truth (Moroni 7:3); when a person dies firm in the faith, passes through the veil of death, and takes up residence in paradise (Alma 40:12); when a person enters the presence of the Lord (D&C 84:24; JST, Exodus 34:2); or when a person is admitted into heaven (Moroni 7:3), what we as Latter-day Saints know as the celestial kingdom.

Resurrection. Just as death is the separation of the spirit from the body, so resurrection is the inseparable reuniting of the spirit and the body (2 Nephi 9:13; Alma 11:43; 40:23). The embodied spirit constitutes the soul of man, and the resurrection is the redemption of that soul (D&C 88:15–16). The fulness of joy comes only through the resurrection (D&C 93:33). Jesus Christ broke the bands of death and was raised from the tomb into celestial, resurrected glory, and because he rose, we have the assurance that each and every mortal will thereby enjoy the immortality of the soul (1 Corinthians 15:21–22; Alma 11:40–42).

Resurrection, first. The first resurrection is the resurrection of those who inherit either celestial or terrestrial glory (Mosiah 15:21–22). The first resurrection, which was initiated in the meridian of time by Jesus Christ, will resume when the Savior returns in glory and will continue throughout the Millennium. Though the phrases are not found in scripture, we often speak colloquially of the morning of the first resurrection as the resurrection of the celestial and the afternoon of the first resurrection as the resurrection of the terrestrial.

Resurrection, last (second). The last, or second, resurrection is the resurrection of those who inherit the telestial glory and those who inherit a kingdom of no glory, the sons of perdition (Mosiah 15:26; D&C 76:81–106; 88:32–35). The second resurrection takes place after the Millennium.

Salvation. To gain salvation, in the scriptural sense, is to gain eternal life (Alma 11:40; D&C 6:13; 14:7). To be saved is to be healed spiritually, to be delivered from death, hell, the devil, and endless torment. Joseph Smith taught that to be saved is to triumph over all our enemies and put them under our feet (*Joseph Smith* [manual], 212). Salvation "consists in the glory, authority, majesty, power and dominion which Jehovah possesses and in nothing else; and no being can possess it but himself or one like him" (*Lectures on Faith*, 76).

Scattering of Israel. The people of Israel, as individuals or as a nation, are scattered when they reject the true Messiah, the gospel covenant, his doctrine, and his church (2 Nephi 6:8–11; 9:1–2; 10:3–7). Israel is also scattered when God chooses, in his eternal wisdom, to relocate a branch of Israel (such as the Lehite colony) so that the promises made to Abraham, Isaac, and Jacob that their posterity would be found throughout the earth and be a blessing to the world may be fulfilled (1 Nephi 17:36–38; 2 Nephi 1:5; 10:20–22).

Sea of glass. The sea of glass spoken of by John in Revelation 4:6 is "the earth, in its sanctified, immortal, and eternal state" (D&C 77:1). It is not that those who inherit the celestial kingdom will literally live on glass but rather that the earth will become like a great urim and thummim (D&C 130:9). That is, those who inhabit the sanctified earth will be "full of the knowledge of the Lord, as the waters cover the sea" (Isaiah 11:9; Habakkuk 2:14).

Second Comforter. The First Comforter is the Holy Ghost, the third member of the Godhead, the One sent of the Father as a comforter, revelator, testator, sanctifier, and sealer (John 14:26; D&C 36:2; 42:17; 50:14). The Second Comforter is the second member of the Godhead, the Lord Jesus Christ himself (John 14:16; *History of the Church*, 3:381). When a person receives the Second Comforter, he or she is brought into the presence of the Lord. The Saints have been taught that such a transcendent privilege, though rare, is possible in this life (D&C 67:10–13; 76:114–18; 88:68; 93:1). Until that glorious day, we are instructed to "seek the face of the Lord always, that in patience ye may possess your souls, and ye shall have eternal life" (D&C 101:38). Inasmuch as the Savior will dwell with his people on earth during the thousand years of peace and joy (3 Nephi 20:22; 21:25), the Millennium is in very deed the day of the Second Comforter.

Second Coming. Although the Lord Jesus Christ will come to earth to visit his people on several occasions before the Millennium, we usually speak of the Second Coming as the time when he comes to all, in glory and in might and majesty and power (Matthew 16:27). He will cleanse the earth of sin and inaugurate an era of peace and righteousness (2 Thessalonians 2:8).

Second comings. Three preliminary comings of the Savior to the earth are spoken of in scripture: his appearance at his temple in Independence, Missouri (Malachi 3:1; D&C 36:8; 42:35–36; 133:2); his appearance at the Council of Adam-ondi-Ahman (D&C 116); and his appearance to the Jews on the Mount of Olives (Zechariah 12:10; 13:6; D&C 45:47–53). Surely there will be other visits, even many visits, to prepare the earth and the Saints of the Most High for their glorious transfiguration.

Spirit prison. See *Hell* in this glossary.

Telestial kingdom. The telestial kingdom is the lowest of the three degrees of glory. It will be made up of those who received neither the testimony of Jesus nor the gospel covenant (D&C 76:82, 101), persons who were divisive, who were liars, adulterers, sorcerers, and murderers, and who defied the laws and statutes of morality and decency (D&C 76:103). Those who inherit the glory of the telestial kingdom will have spent the Millennium in the postmortal spirit world being cleansed of their sins and made ready for this lowest kingdom of glory, whose glory "surpasses all understanding" (D&C 76:89).

Terrestrial kingdom. The terrestrial kingdom is likened to the glory of the moon in contrast to the celestial kingdom, which is likened to the glory of the sun (D&C 76:78). Those who inherit the terrestrial kingdom are they "who received not the testimony of Jesus in the flesh, but afterwards [in the postmortal spirit world] received it"; because they are not then "valiant in the testimony of Jesus," they do not qualify for a celestial crown (D&C 76:74, 79). Inhabitants of the terrestrial kingdom will thus be the honorable men and women of the earth who lived the best lives they knew to live, but because they are not valiant in the testimony of Jesus once they receive it, they do not qualify for the richer blessings associated with living the celestial law.

Transfiguration of the earth. When Christ returns in glory, the earth and all who abide its presence will be transfigured, that is, raised to a higher spiritual plain for a season (D&C 63:20–21). More specifically, they are raised from a telestial to a terrestrial glory (Articles of Faith 1:10).

Translated beings. The Prophet Joseph Smith taught that translated beings, such as Enoch, Moses, Elijah, John the Beloved, and the Three Nephites, have been raised to a terrestrial order (*Teachings of the Prophet Joseph Smith,* 170). As such, they are not subject to distress, pain, or death, but because they have not yet passed through death and the resurrection, they are still mortal, albeit in a glorified mortal condition.

Zion. Zion is the highest order of priesthood society and also the abode of the pure in heart, which is any place where the pure in heart dwell (D&C 97:21). While the center stake of Zion, or the New Jerusalem, will eventually be established in Independence, Jackson County, Missouri (D&C 57:3), Zion will be any place a stake is formed and operating. At the time of the Lord's coming in glory, the Zion from above (Enoch's Zion and, presumably, Melchizedek's city of Salem) will unite with Zion on earth in a grand and sacred reunion (JST, Genesis 14:25–40; D&C 84:100; Moses 7:62–65).

SOURCES

Andrus, Hyrum L., and Helen Mae Andrus, comps. *They Knew the Prophet*. Salt Lake City: Deseret Book, 1999.

Augustine. *The City of God*. Translated by Marcus Dods. Peabody, MA: Hendrickson Publishers, 2009.

[Ballard, Melvin R.] *Melvin J. Ballard—Crusader for Righteousness*. Salt Lake City: Bookcraft, 1966.

Ballard, M. Russell. "When Shall These Things Be?" In *Brigham Young University 1995–96 Speeches*, 185–93. Provo, UT: Brigham Young University, 1996.

Benson, Ezra Taft. *The Teachings of Ezra Taft Benson*. Salt Lake City: Bookcraft, 1988.

Cannon, George Q. *Gospel Truth: Discourses and Writings of George Q. Cannon*. 2 vols. in 1. Edited by Jerreld L. Newquist. Salt Lake City: Deseret Book, 1987.

Hinckley, Gordon B. "As One Who Loves the Prophet." In *Joseph Smith: The Prophet, the Man*, edited by Susan Easton Black and Charles D. Tate Jr., 1–13. Provo, UT: BYU Religious Studies Center, 1993.

———. *Be Thou an Example*. Salt Lake City: Deseret Book, 1981.

———. *Teachings of Gordon B. Hinckley*. Salt Lake City: Deseret Book, 1997.

Holland, Jeffrey R. *Christ and the New Covenant: The Messianic Message of the Book of Mormon*. Salt Lake City: Deseret Book, 1997.

Hunter, Howard W. *The Teachings of Howard W. Hunter*. Edited by Clyde J. Williams. Salt Lake City: Bookcraft, 1997.

Hymns of The Church of Jesus Christ of Latter-day Saints. Salt Lake City: The Church of Jesus Christ of Latter-day Saints, 1985.

Journal of Discourses. 26 vols. Liverpool: Latter-day Saints' Book Depot, 1854–86.

Kimball, Spencer W. *The Miracle of Forgiveness.* Salt Lake City: Bookcraft, 1969.

———. *The Teachings of Spencer W. Kimball.* Edited by Edward L. Kimball. Salt Lake City: Bookcraft, 1982.

Lectures on Faith. Salt Lake City: Deseret Book, 1985.

Maxwell, Neal A. *Even As I Am.* Salt Lake City: Deseret Book, 1982.

———. *Wherefore, Ye Must Press Forward.* Salt Lake City: Deseret Book, 1977.

———. *A Wonderful Flood of Light.* Salt Lake City: Bookcraft, 1990.

McConkie, Bruce R. *Doctrinal New Testament Commentary.* 3 vols. Salt Lake City: Bookcraft, 1965–73.

———. "Jesus Christ and Him Crucified." In *1976 Devotional Speeches of the Year: BYU Bicentennial Devotional and Fireside Addresses,* 391–405. Provo, UT: Brigham Young University Press, 1977.

———. *The Millennial Messiah: The Second Coming of the Son of Man.* Salt Lake City: Deseret Book, 1982.

———. *A New Witness for the Articles of Faith.* Salt Lake City: Deseret Book, 1985.

———. *The Promised Messiah.* Salt Lake City: Deseret Book, 1978.

Nelson, Russell M. *Perfection Pending and Other Favorite Discourses.* Salt Lake City: Deseret Book, 1998.

Oaks, Dallin H. *With Full Purpose of Heart.* Salt Lake City: Deseret Book, 2002.

Packer, Boyd K. *Mine Errand from the Lord: Selections from the Sermons and Writings of Boyd K. Packer.* Compiled by Clyde J. Williams. Salt Lake City: Deseret Book, 2008.

Penrose, Charles W. *"Mormon" Doctrine, Plain and Simple; or, Leaves from the Tree of Life.* 2nd ed. Salt Lake City: Geo. Q. Cannon & Sons, 1897.

———. "The Second Advent." *Latter-day Saints' Millennial Star* 21, no. 37 (10 Sept. 1859): 581–96.

Pratt, Orson. *Masterful Discourses and Writings of Orson Pratt.* Salt Lake City: Bookcraft, 1962.

Romney, Marion G. "The Light Shineth." *Ensign,* Dec. 1971, 75–77.

———. Conference Report, Oct. 1965, 20–23.

Smith, Joseph. "Correspondence." *Times and Seasons* 4, no. 8 (1 Mar. 1843): 113–28.

———. *History of The Church of Jesus Christ of Latter-day Saints*. Edited by B. H. Roberts. 7 vols. 2nd ed. rev. Salt Lake City: The Church of Jesus Christ of Latter-day Saints, 1932–51.

———. *Joseph Smith* [manual]. Teachings of Presidents of the Church series. Salt Lake City: The Church of Jesus Christ of Latter-day Saints, 2007.

———. *Teachings of the Prophet Joseph Smith*. Selected by Joseph Fielding Smith. Salt Lake City: Deseret Book, 1976.

———. "A Vision." *Times and Seasons* 4, no. 6 (1 Feb. 1843): 81–96.

———. *The Words of Joseph Smith: The Contemporary Accounts of the Nauvoo Discourses of the Prophet Joseph*. Compiled and edited by Andrew F. Ehat and Lyndon W. Cook. Provo, UT: BYU Religious Studies Center, 1980.

Smith, Joseph F. *Gospel Doctrine*. Salt Lake City: Deseret Book, 1971.

———. "Redemption beyond the Grave." *Improvement Era* 5, no. 2 (Dec. 1901): 81–160.

Smith, Joseph Fielding. *Doctrines of Salvation*. Compiled by Bruce R. McConkie. 3 vols. Salt Lake City: Bookcraft, 1954–56.

———. *Man: His Origin and Destiny*. Salt Lake City: Deseret Book, 1954.

———. *The Progress of Man*. Salt Lake City: Deseret Book, 1964.

———. *The Signs of the Times*. Salt Lake City: Deseret Book, 1952.

———. *The Way to Perfection*. Salt Lake City: Deseret Book, 1970.

Snow, Lorenzo. *Lorenzo Snow* [manual]. Teachings of Presidents of the Church series. Salt Lake City: The Church of Jesus Christ of Latter-day Saints, 2012.

Whitney, Orson F. *Life of Heber C. Kimball*. Salt Lake City: Bookcraft, 1973.

Wilkinson, Bruce, and David Kopp. *A Life God Rewards*. Sisters, OR: Multnomah Publishers, 2002.

Young, Brigham. "The Resurrection." *Elders' Journal* 1, no. 12 (July 1904): 149–68.

SCRIPTURE INDEX

SUBJECT INDEX